To Chelse

MW00626205

# BoLD

## & COURAGEOUS

How to Confidently &

Unapologetically Walk in Your

God-Given Authority

*May you be more bold and*
*courageous with your life, story,*
*and voice! You were born to*
*shift the world & I pray*
*you walk in that power!*

## CANDACE JUNÉE ARMOUR

Published by
ELOHAI International Publishing & Media
P.O. Box 1883
Cypress, Texas 77410
www.elohaiintl.com

Scriptures marked AMP are taken from the AMPLIFIED® BIBLE, Copyright © 1954, 1958, 1962, 1964, 1965, 1987 by the Lockman Foundation. Used by Permission. (www.Lockman.org)

Scriptures marked BSB are taken from The Holy Bible, Berean Study Bible, BSB Copyright © 2016, 2020 by Bible Hub Used by Permission. All Rights Reserved Worldwide.

Scriptures marked CEV are taken from the CONTEMPORARY ENGLISH VERSION (CEV) copyright © 1995 by the American Bible Society. Used by permission.

Scriptures marked ESV are taken from the THE HOLY BIBLE, ENGLISH STANDARD VERSION (ESV)® Copyright © 2001 by Crossway, a publishing ministry of Good News Publishers. Used by permission.

Scriptures marked NLT are taken from THE HOLY BIBLE, NEW LIVING TRANSLATION (NLT): Copyright © 1996, 2004, 2007 by Tyndale House Foundation. Used by permission of Tyndale House Publishers, Inc., Carol Stream, Illinois 60188. All rights reserved. Used by permission.

Scriptures marked NIV are taken from THE HOLY BIBLE, NEW INTERNATIONAL VERSION®. Copyright © 1973, 1978, 1984, 2011 by Biblica, Inc.™. Used by permission of Zondervan.

Scriptures marked NKJV are taken from the NEW KING JAMES VERSION®. Copyright © 1982 by Thomas Nelson, Inc.

Scriptures marked TLB are taken from THE LIVING BIBLE (TLB) copyright © 1971. Used by permission of Tyndale House Publishers, Inc., Carol Stream, Illinois 60188. All rights reserved. Used by permission. All rights reserved.

ISBN: 978-1-953535-70-2

Printed in the United States of America

# Dedication

To my mother, whom I love deeply, thank you. You allowed me to share our story and my truth so that others can heal and become more *Bold & Courageous*. You instilled faith in me to believe in the God of the Bible, to value education, and to never give up. You birthed and cared for four children day in and day out. You made sure that our family consistently had a home-cooked meal, made sure we had clean clothes to wear to school and work, and took time to take us shopping for school necessities year after year. You picked my siblings and me up from school sports, you cheered us on in the stands, and you drove hours and even out of state to celebrate significant milestones and tournaments. You made sacrifices to make sure your kids had cell phones. You spent summers teaching us phonics, grammar, and math — and even went out of your way to make sure we had good times swimming at the local pool. You made sure your kids knew Jesus, by driving us to church faithfully every Sunday — even if you had to get four kids ready and take them to church alone. You prayed for our family consistently throughout the years. You've been a phenomenal mother, and your life deserves to be celebrated. You've taught me thousands of lessons, and I'm so grateful to have been blessed with a mother like you. You've shaped me into the woman I've become, and for that, I'm forever grateful. I love you.

# Contents

# Acknowledgments

This book has been a long time coming and has shown me a side of myself I never knew existed. Thank you to all those who made it possible: to the amazing women of the Epic Fab Girl community, Allison, Cassie, Iman, Latisha, and Raliat who thoroughly reviewed the first draft of this book and provided thoughtful feedback. To one of my very best friends, Dr. Tiffany N. Ford, who believed in, supported, pushed, and invested in me to make this book a reality. To my friend and sister in Christ, Taylor Michele Bell, who inspired the title of this book. To my client turned book coach, Nikkie Pryce, for pushing me to share the most real, raw, and even uncomfortable parts of my journey to help others become bold and courageous. To my biological siblings who have loved and supported me through tough times and reminded me that my words are valuable and needed. Thank you. I love each of you dearly.

And I want to thank me. *Snoop Dog voice* I want to thank me for believing in me, doing the hard work, and never quitting. For sacrificing to make this happen. But seriously...

Above all, I am so thankful to God for giving me the ability to articulate my thoughts and story in this way. Without God, my life is meaningless. I'm forever grateful to God for carrying me, healing me, restoring me, keeping me, and fighting for me through the years. My life has never been the same since I surrendered my life and exchanged my plans for His ultimate will. To God be the glory. This one is for you, Yahweh.

# Introduction

In high school, I was the kid that was popular by accident. I made no attempt to be popular. I just genuinely wanted to know people and make friends as a freshman, so I met a ton of people and was friendly to everyone I grew to know.

I went to a pretty big high school with around 1,000 students in my freshman class. Every year, the students in each class would nominate people that they thought deserved the coveted sash for homecoming court — king and queen. They'd narrow down the top entries to four people, and the winner would be announced during the homecoming pep rally.

Freshman year, to my surprise, I was nominated for homecoming court. I was shocked and nervous, but it made it a little better that I was nominated alongside three of my closest friends. To me, that meant I wouldn't have to go through this experience alone. I was excited for myself and for my friends as well. This was a good thing, right? What happened next was something I wish I would have paid a lot more attention to as a teenager.

After anxiously waiting, the day of the pep rally finally arrived. I dressed up in a fancy outfit and heels, styled my hair and makeup to look my best, and I showed up alongside my girlfriends. They sat us in a row of chairs as we anxiously awaited the words: "This year's freshman homecoming court winner is…"

I sat there with my heart racing. I thought of all the reasons why all the other girls deserved the sash more than me. All my friends on homecoming court were smart, pretty, and sociable so it was all up in the air. Who would get the sash?

With the entire student body of over 4,000 students watching and waiting, they announced… "This year's freshman homecoming court winner is: Candace Armour."

The crowd went into a FRENZY. They didn't know what they wanted to do — there was some excitement, but there were also some unrecognizable sounds. All I can remember is my body locking up with anxiety and reminding myself not to trip as I walked across the gymnasium floor from one side of the basketball court to the other. Remember, I was a freshman in heels — I hadn't truly mastered the art of walking in heels and that's all I could think of.

The male winner came over to escort me across the floor and we started our trek to the other end of the basketball court. As we took the first step, my thoughts of not tripping were interrupted with booing from the crowd. I nervously walked across that gymnasium floor as the upperclassmen booed us because we were freshmen. The shouts of excitement from the 1,000 members of the freshman class were drowned out by the upperclassmen.

All I could think was, "Wow, I won…. I can't wait to get back to my seat. This is embarrassing." But I still had to push through and try my best not to crumble. It was rough, and quite honestly, traumatizing. I didn't realize the impact of that traumatic experience until much later in life.

Imagine thinking for so many years that your wins are embarrassing and shouldn't be celebrated. Imagine feeling like you needed to dull your shine because of others' responses to your existence and your wins. That was me. The girl who tried to shift herself to make others feel comfortable.

Candace Junée today? She's *Bold & Courageous*… confident and unapologetic.

I am a full-time entrepreneur who serves women in different capacities. I run a brand, Epic Fab Girl, for go-getters and Christian women entrepreneurs helping them build profitable brands and grow their faith. I also run a marketing consulting business, Candace Junée Marketing, where I help women master their marketing and build six-figure businesses and beyond.

I am a social media content creator on Instagram, TikTok, and YouTube. I am blessed to be an international speaker and world traveler. In school I studied mechanical engineering and received a Master of Business Administration with a concentration in marketing and accounting. I've accomplished a lot in my thirty years of life, and I've also learned so much about myself and the world.

Over the years, as I've journeyed to become the *Bold &
Courageous* woman I am today. I have grown to be much
more confident. There were many lessons along the way that
brought me here. I had to fight hard to get here. While I do
not know everything, I'm sharing my story, wisdom, and lessons with you.

This book is aimed to help you shift from thoughts of
inadequacy and timidity to unapologetically owning your
brilliance, expertise, and God-given authority. It will challenge you to look deep within yourself. At times you may
experience anxiety, fear, frustration — and you might even
shed a tear. You might even have to put the book down for
a while just to process what is coming up. But promise me
that you will bring your full self to this experience as you read
this book.

Throughout this book, I'll share personal stories and accounts
of real-life experiences. Many of the names of people in the
book have been changed to protect their identities.

Though I took a few psychology classes in high school and
college, let's be clear that I am not giving professional advice
for your mental health and well-being. I am absolutely an
advocate of professional therapy and counseling. I recommend that as you read this book and uncover areas that you
need to sort out and heal from, that you take your findings
to a professional who can help you receive the healing and
mental health experience that you deserve.

In this book, I cover topics that may trigger past trauma,
including sexual assault, domestic violence, and depression.

If you or someone you know needs assistance, here are a few resources to help:

Suicide Prevention Hotline: 1-800-273-8255
Domestic Violence Hotline: 1-800-799-7233
National Sexual Assault Hotline: 1-800-656-4673

After reading this book, the goal is for you to be even more *Bold & Courageous* than you were before. Let's define what both of those looks like according to the Google dictionary.

**Bold /bōld/**: showing an ability to take risks; confident and courageous.

**Courageous /kəˈrājəs/:** not deterred by danger or pain; brave.

I'm now inviting you on the journey to confidently take risks and not be deterred by danger or pain. That's where the best version of you exists.

Our world is desperately waiting for the best version of you to show up. But first, you need to face your most vulnerable self so you can become the version of you that you were always destined to be.

# 1 *Bold & Courageous Vision*

If you ask anyone who knows me well, they'd describe me as driven, focused, fearless, motivated, and ambitious. Have I always made bold decisions? Yes *and no*; it's complicated. Have I always been courageous? No, but courage has to be built.

I am going to share with you how I've become courageous over the years and what motivates me to take such bold decisions.

In reality, though I'm a courageous person, I do not claim to be fearless. The way my brain works, I'm an extremely calculated person. I'm the type of person who usually imagines every possible scenario — and that's where fear creeps in.

But here's the thing. Fear does not stop me from doing what I'm driven and motivated to do. There are times when fear gets the best of me, but I have learned to be courageous in the face of fear so that my fear takes a backseat to my courage.

Growing up in Chicago, I was the child who was the unintentional overachiever. I was good at most things I tried. If

I attempted to do something I wasn't good at, my ambition carried me through until I mastered being good at that, too.

I've always had my hand in a lot of things. I could dance, play softball, style hair, write well, perform theatre, play the violin, but I could never sing very well (lol). I was a math whiz — I loved it. I enjoyed learning, and I became good at it. I was a straight-A student who was often awarded for my achievement.

Somehow, I managed to have a blossoming social life. I was graced to be able to hang out with the self-proclaimed nerds and the popular crew, and somehow my personality always fit in. I was somewhat of a unicorn.

My father was a high achiever, too. Everything he did was with a hustle mentality. My father was a full-time entrepreneur ever since I knew him. He started his business the year after I was born. My dad was the breadwinner in my family, so entrepreneurship was all I ever knew.

I didn't really understand the impact of what my dad had built until I got much older. However, I watched my dad (who was not a college graduate) build a wildly successful business from the ground up from what he learned in trade school.

My father's achievements in business supported my family financially and provided a seemingly well-rounded life where we never really had to experience financial lack.

Both my mom and dad were Chicago natives who valued education. My mother was a teacher growing up, so she made sure we spent our summers getting ahead with

"Hooked on Phonics" and math equations. I hated it. All I cared about was going swimming, but she wouldn't let us play outside or go swimming until all of our summer coursework she assigned us for the day was complete.

If you know anything about the city of Chicago and its public education system, then you know that your school was determined by where you lived. My parents always wanted us to attend the best schools, but it wasn't that easy to do in Chicago.

We lived in a small, somewhat diverse, neighborhood on Chicago's south side, and the schools in our neighborhood were alright, but they were not the best schools the city had to offer. There was an option to go to better public schools despite where you lived, but you had to test into them to have a better education. Every year when the test time came around, my mom would make sure my siblings and I tested to see if we could make the cut to be considered "gifted" to be accepted into one of the city's top-performing schools.

And then one year came around and I tested into the "gifted" program. My mom was able to find a school that had space for me in their gifted program, and it also allowed siblings of the gifted students to attend their standard program.

The schools my siblings and I had previously attended were pretty diverse with students and teachers of several racial backgrounds. The only gifted program that had space for me in it was in the heart of Chicago's south side. Beasley Academic Center was located right in front of the Robert Taylor Housing Projects and in the middle of a majority black community. That meant the school was nearly 100 percent black. The school's culture there was just different, and it was wildly different from the school experience we had previously.

I was excited to start a new school and even more excited when I learned that the school had a swimming pool. What I thought would be an exciting experience turned into a nightmare I wouldn't have wished on any fourth grader.

I was the new kid and I looked different. I was one of very few light-skinned kids in the class and my classmates were convinced that I was white. Even when I insisted that both of my parents were black, they tried to figure out which parent of mine was *really* white. Growing up I had always been called "light-bright" or "yellow" by family and others I knew, but never white. This was new and made me very uncomfortable. My classmates were confused about why I looked the way I looked, and it turned into teasing because I was different.

Not only did my classmates call me white, but they made fun of my body size and the shape of my nose. They teased me, called me ugly, and called me "Ms. Piggy" saying that I looked like her because of my nose and body. As a fourth grader, being called a Muppet was ridiculously traumatizing. For years, I hated my nose and was convinced that I was ugly because that's what my classmates said.

I remember feeling so alone in that school. Feeling like what I thought would be an amazing experience turned into the first place I ever really had to consistently be on the defense.

Beasley was the type of school where fights broke out often and the cool kids were praised for being mean. There were times when I was bullied to the point of fighting.

I'll never forget the day I learned that I could fight. We would take bathroom breaks as a class. Everyone would line up in single-file order and we were limited to only two-to-three students in the bathroom at a time. The teacher would wait outside to monitor the rest of the class. That day was no different.

I went into the bathroom and after I left the bathroom stall, I realized I was left alone with one of the mean girls from my class. She cornered me and slurred something mean in my direction. With no adult supervision in sight, I got enough courage to say something back in defense of myself. Next thing you know... there we were, fighting. The fight ended with me pinning her against the wall and telling her to NEVER put her hands on me ever again. After that, she left me alone. I'm sure she never told her friends what happened out of embarrassment.

I was a kind, sensitive girl who was now forced to defend herself constantly. Ironically enough, despite all the drama that I experienced in fourth grade, I looked forward to the days the class spent at the swimming pool. I was one of about three students in my class of about thirty "gifted" students who actually knew how to swim. The majority of the class would be in the shallow end of the pool because they couldn't swim, or they were too afraid to venture into the deep end. I found myself being excited to separate from them while jumping off the diving board and treading water. It was the place where I found peace during my day.

Swimming at Beasley taught me that even the toughest, brightest people have fears that traumatize them. Even bullies are afraid of something. I'll share more on fear later, but for now, we'll stick to my terrible experience as a ten-year-old.

I dreaded going to school, so when my parents announced that we were moving to the suburbs and starting at a new school, I was ecstatic! There was hope that my experience would get better!

Over the years I've learned to adjust to new environments – good and bad. Many of them are scary on-sight, but I've learned how to conquer as best I know how.

Whether you're moving to a new school or standing up against a bully, courage is necessary to overcome tough situations. Courage often comes when you're tired of experiencing the environment that a lack of courage creates. Courage often comes when you're fed up or completely sick and tired. Courage often comes when you're tired of being taken advantage of, overlooked, or even misunderstood.

I don't believe that any of us have the courage we need to overcome when we take the first step to overcome. When we first encounter that mountain that seems impossible to face, we have to build our courage. I believe that courage comes during the journey. Whether the journey takes us through the mountain, over the mountain, around the mountain, or you become so fed up with the mountain that you speak to the mountain and tell it to move, you need courage to face it.

Having the courage to take the first step is often the hardest part, but courage grows when you take that first step and it isn't as scary as you thought it would be. Courage grows more when you experience the beauty and relief that comes with making bold decisions despite your fears.

You, my friend, deserve to be courageous. You deserve to speak to mountains and tell them to move.

Now, let's get into the premise of this book. I'm going to take you to one of my favorite verses in the Bible to lay the foundation for the rest of this book: Joshua 1:9.

Let me set the stage for you, first. In the Bible, we are told that Moses led the children of Israel out of captivity from Pharaoh's rule in Egypt. The children of Israel were previously enslaved, but God promised them a new life in the Promised Land, a land of milk and honey.

The land of milk and honey represented abundance and overflow. It was God's promise to His people. One thing about God, when He makes a promise, it becomes a covenant that we can trust. God's promise to them was to shift them from slavery into overflow.

After Moses died, God spoke to Joshua saying:

> "Moses my servant is dead. Now then, you and all these people, get ready to cross the Jordan River into the land I am about to give to them — to the Israelites. I will

give you every place where you set your foot, as I promised Moses. Your territory will extend from the desert
to Lebanon, and from the great river, the Euphrates
— all the Hittite country — to the Mediterranean Sea
in the west. No one will be able to stand against you
all the days of your life. As I was with Moses, so I will
be with you; I will never leave you nor forsake you.
Be strong and courageous, because you will lead these
people to inherit the land I swore to their ancestors to
give them" (Joshua 1:2-6 NIV).

At this point, the children of Israel's trusted leader, Moses,
had died and God appointed Joshua as the new leader who
would take the children of Israel into the promised land.

Let's put ourselves in Joshua's shoes. Imagine being forced to
take on a leadership role when you have no other option but
to go into a new territory. Whether or not you thought you
were ready to face this new feat you had to face it. You had
to figure it out.

Imagine being crippled by the thoughts of fear of the unknown.
Imagine crumbling at the thought of failing the people who
you're leading. Imagine the amount of pressure of having to
take on such a big task. Since you're reading this book, I know
you've been there before, and you can probably relate.

You know what it feels like to be overwhelmed with the weight
of the assignment before you. You know what it feels like to
have to chart a path that has never been taken. You know what
it feels like to be scared about the unknown, but still have to
take a step forward.

That's exactly the point where we find Joshua. God told him to be strong and courageous in verse six, but he repeated himself again in verse seven, and again in Joshua 1:9. Let's take a look at this verse:

> "'Have I not commanded you? Be strong and courageous. Do not be afraid; do not be discouraged, for the LORD your God will be with you wherever you go' (Joshua 1:9 NIV)."

Something tells me that Joshua paused, or even halted, before he moved forward. Simply by the way that God spoke to him saying, "Have I not commanded you?," It was almost as if he had to tell him twice just so he could take action. It was almost as if Joshua had not moved immediately upon instruction.

I believe what the Bible says about God. I believe that He is all-knowing, all-powerful, and that He knows our thoughts. God knew exactly what was on Joshua's mind. We will never know if Joshua's mind was filled with thoughts of inadequacy, thoughts of fear, or thoughts of trying to figure out the step-by-step strategy to get into the promised land. But what we do know is that God made it clear that he should be strong and courageous. He also made it clear that it was a command — Joshua had no other choice.

Another version of this verse says:

> "Yes, be bold and strong! Banish fear and doubt! For remember, the Lord your God is with you wherever you go" (Joshua 1:9 TLB).

Joshua was challenged by God to be both bold and courageous. Today, I'm challenging you to be both bold and courageous, too.

Throughout the rest of this text, we will dig even deeper into Joshua 1, specifically focusing our attention on Joshua 1:9.

This is one of my favorite bible verses because I've experienced so much fear in my life. I have struggled with anxiety throughout my life, and for years I never knew it. Now that I'm more self-aware, I understand the impact of fear and anxiety on my life. I've been able to pull on this verse in moments when I know I'm being challenged to make courageous decisions.

I've done some considerably courageous things in my life:

- I quit my six-figure job in corporate America with no consistent source of income to support myself.
- I traveled to Mexico by myself for four months during a pandemic.
- I shared with the world on social media that I experienced rape (prior to the #MeToo movement).
- I bought my first house at twenty-five years old.
- I spoke publicly at my first Go-Getter Conference even though I had an intense fear of public speaking.

I've grown to make these courageous decisions because, like Joshua, I recognize that God will be with me wherever I go. But that doesn't mean I did not experience fear. I feel fear all the time, but I have learned how to take courageous steps of faith regardless of what my mind tells me.

When I went away to college at Washington University in St. Louis, I had big dreams of being successful. For the longest time, I had no idea how to hone in on one thing to focus on in school. I was torn between focusing my studies on business or taking another path like journalism. I loved to write and speak in front of the camera, so I just knew one of these paths would be right for me.

In 2009, Washington University was ranked as the #12 university in the nation at the time. When I initially applied to Washington University, I indicated that I wanted to study business. I was accepted to attend; however, my acceptance was contingent upon my performance in their Freshman Summer Academic Program. My standardized test scores on my ACT were lower than the school's average, so the school made it clear that they wanted me to be a part of their summer program to prove that I could keep up with the academic rigor.

Not only was I conditionally accepted, but I was also not admitted in the school's undergraduate business program. I remember feeling so upset because I had finally nailed down what I wanted to focus on and now I was completely lost. I felt like I was going into college having to prove myself, and my self-esteem took a blow because of it.

I spent the summer before my freshman year trying to figure out what path to take and one of my friends helped me land on mechanical engineering. I loved calculus and physics, so it made lots of sense at the time.

I made it through that summer and successfully completed the program. Once officially on campus in the fall, I was able to keep up academically for the most part. There was one time during my college career when I had to withdraw from Calculus 3 because I would have failed if I had continued at the same rate I was going. I was admitted into the school with a contingency, and I wondered if Washington University had made the right decision to bet on me. I talked to a few friends about my decision, and they encouraged me to know that just because I was struggling in the moment it didn't mean I was a failure. I could always try again in the future. When I dropped out of that class, I felt a huge relief. I also made up in my mind that I belonged on that campus regardless of how I got into the school, and I would not allow myself to believe I was incapable because of it. I ended up taking Calculus 3 in the future and did well. I've learned to extend myself grace in the journey and understand that my accomplishments and failures do not define me.

Though I loved calculus and physics, by my junior year I realized engineering was not the career path I wanted to take. I had chosen to study engineering because I knew it would help me land a job after college and I knew I could get through the coursework.

During my junior year of college, I decided to switch gears and study business, one of my real passions. I applied for Wash U's MBA program and was accepted to attend their "3-2 Program". This program would allow me to spend my senior year and one additional year taking on business coursework to get my Master of Business Administration degree.

I had finally won. For the first time ever, I sat in classrooms that excited me. I was eager to learn more about business and thrilled that the same school who had denied me entry into their undergraduate business program had offered me a spot in their MBA program.

Not only was it a big deal to me, but it was also a big deal for my family. My dad had two children prior to marrying my mom, both of which had matriculated through college and received degrees. My mom and dad had four children together, and I was their third child together. Of my parents' four children, my two older siblings had gone away to college but hadn't yet received college degrees at the time.

By the time I was entering into my fourth year in school, I was now the only one of my parents' children that was still on track to complete my degree in four years. This meant that I would be the first of my parents' children to receive a college degree, and when I graduated, I would graduate with not just one degree, but two. Remember, education was extremely important to my parents, so they were very excited and proud of me.

I'm the kid that my parents bragged about to friends and family, and even strangers. I know because it was embarrassing, at times. They'd pull me into conversations to tell people what I was up to or what I had accomplished. They were proud parents. So, their excitement for my new academic endeavors was nothing new. I had been on the Honor Roll for years and received many awards for my school achievements.

I believe that in my parents' minds, I was their kid that got things right when it came to my education. By the time I graduated in 2014, I landed a job in corporate America making over $70,000 a year straight out of undergrad. That was yet another thing for my parents to feel proud of and brag about. For that reason, I'm not even sure I shared my salary with my family when I received my offer.

After graduation, I was off to working my new job in the consulting industry as a digital marketing analyst. About a year and a half into this job, I grew uninterested, dissatisfied, burnt out, and just plain old tired. While the money I was making was great, I wasn't passionate about the work I was doing. I had so many perks of being able to travel across the country and rack up hotel and flight points, but it wasn't worth my feelings of discontent.

Shortly after starting my job, I realized that I would often be expected to work late nights, catch up on work on weekends, and even go above and beyond to get my work done. I would transition from one project at the company to another. Some projects were fun and gave me the space to have a flexible schedule and others required me to work sixteen-hour days just to get the job done. It was draining, but for a while it was manageable.

This is until the dreaded fall season of 2016 came around. Everything at work started to go downhill from there. I ended up on a remote project with a manager who had completely unrealistic expectations of me. On top of that, he spoke very condescending toward me. The project was a disaster, and I was not equipped with the tools to be successful in the role. It got to a point where my manager would micro-manage my work and schedule daily calls with me to review my work for the day as if I were a child.

The pressure placed on me in that role was ridiculous. I would have to get up to meet with my team at 6 a.m., work all day, and then have calls with our teammates in India from 10 to 11 p.m. There was no work-life balance on top of me not knowing what the heck I was doing on the job. I worked from home, from my bed daily.

Amid the chaos, I had a conversation with my manager where he completely disrespected me. It made me feel so uncomfortable and I communicated with his manager (a woman) on the project who I thought would help facilitate and make the situation better. When that didn't happen, I just suffered through it in hopes that I could get through the project until it ended.

There was daily pressure to get caught up on work, get ahead, and meet deadlines set in place by leadership. In my manager's eyes, every hour, every minute, and every second of my time was crucial to the success of this project.

Then one morning while on the project, I received a phone call from my mom. She was hysterical. I could barely make out what she was saying. It was one of the most terrifying, gut-wrenching sounds I've ever heard. "My brother is gone!" she said.

My mother continued to wail, cry, yell, and shout with disbelief. Her brother, my uncle, had passed away suddenly while at work at the age of fifty-one. It was completely unexpected and took my entire family by surprise. My uncle was a pillar in our family, and we were all shocked at his passing.

When I found out about my uncle's death, I immediately collapsed to the ground. My legs buckled underneath me.

All I could think about was how my three cousins had just lost their father and how his wife had just lost her soulmate.

I took a moment to gather myself as much as possible after I got off the phone with my mom. As I frantically packed up my belongings and prepared to leave my house to be with my family at the hospital, I picked up the phone to call my manager. Still frazzled from unexpected grief that hit me like a ton of bricks, I spoke to my manager with my voice trembling and shaking.

Anybody who could have heard my voice would have known I was not well. I told my manager that my uncle had passed away unexpectedly, and I needed to go be with my family. I told him that I was heading to the hospital and was taking the day off. What he said next shocked me, but in some ways it didn't. His only concern was work. There was no compassion or empathy.

He said something along the lines of, "Since you won't be working today, someone else will have to cover the work you're doing. Send me everything you are working on before you leave." Twenty-five year old Candace responded, "Okay" and hurried off the phone.

I proceeded to gather everything I was working on to send it over to my manager. It took me over two hours to organize everything I was working on and email it to my manager so someone could make progress while I was away.

I hopped in my car to head to the hospital and called my mom to let her know I was on my way. My mother told me that everyone had already left the hospital, including my aunt. My heart sank. Everyone had gone their separate ways so I proceeded to drive to my parents' house where my mom would be.

On the forty-five-minute drive to my parents' house, I received a phone call from my manager regarding work even though I communicated that I was taking the day off. We spoke briefly about work, and I answered his pressing questions. By the afternoon, while spending time grieving with my family, I received even more text messages from my manager regarding work.

I could not understand why my manager thought that work was more significant than a family grieving. I could not understand why he was texting my phone.

I was fed up with his insensitivity. So, I stopped responding. Though I wish I would have had the courage to communicate to him that I was not in a position to respond, that day was the last straw for me. That was the day I realized I needed to get out of corporate America sooner than later. That was the day I began to create a vision for my life that looked different than what I'd ever seen or experienced.

Within less than a month I was kicked off that project at work. It basically felt like I was being fired, but I was relieved because I didn't have to deal with a stressful manager anymore.

Throughout my time on that project, I was very open about my faith. My manager eventually publicly apologized for his behavior and poor treatment of me, stating that he was under immense pressure to perform. I courageously forgave him and told him that I still wish nothing but the best for him, despite the pain he had caused me. He was surprised that I extended grace by forgiving him, and I told him that my character was exemplary of the God I serve. He commended me for my strong faith, and we went our separate ways.

I went on to work on a couple of more exciting projects after that, but the work-life balance still presented itself to be a problem.

For one project, I traveled to New York for a fashion-focused project, and I was excited because I had never been to New York City. My excitement to see the city was drowned out by the amount of work that I had to do on the project.

When I arrived to meet my team for the first night, we stayed in the office until 1 a.m. getting our PowerPoint slides ready for the client. The next day we visited the client site, and, to my surprise, we completely scrapped the presentation and didn't even go through the slides during the meeting.

By the time we were done meeting with the client, it was 11 p.m. and time to head back to my hotel. There was no time to see the city because I had to be up at 5:30 a.m. just to get back to the office by 7 a.m.

Project after project, I experienced the same thing. There was no space for work-life balance. While working on one project we had a virtual meeting on a Sunday morning just to prepare for the client. It was ridiculous.

To me, the weekends should be reserved for family and personal time. I grew tired of being in a space where the demands of my job were impacting my mental health, my free-time, and my overall happiness.

During that time, I started to dream of life outside of corporate America. I began to create a vision for my life that looked very different than late nights and early mornings, ridiculous schedules, consistent stress, and no work-life balance.

I realized that entrepreneurship could help me create a life that I loved and have the time freedom and financial freedom that I desperately desired.

The vision for my life included the ability to travel often, the ability to avoid working too many hours in a day, and the ability to work on projects that made me feel fulfilled and see the impact in people's lives. That vision seemed so far away, but I knew that was a possibility for me in the future. That vision was the driving force behind me deciding to quit my job.

When I quit my job, it was a big deal. I was finally getting paid six figures and my family was so excited to know that. However, the money I made was not worth the pain I endured and the freedom I lacked.

I had to quit my job *for me*. It wasn't about anybody else. Not even my family. I had to do what was best for me and my vision for my life. So, when I quit my job in corporate America, I didn't tell my parents… I just did it and haven't looked back ever since.

Quitting my six-figure job in corporate America was one of the scariest things I've ever done, but I couldn't let fear stop me this time. It almost stopped me from quitting, but I made the bold decision to bet on myself. It has paid off over time.

People often ask me how I became so courageous and seemingly fearless, but the truth is that I am not fearless. I just understand that like Joshua in the Bible, my journey to the "Promised Land" is not about me. My journey is about the other people I'm called to serve.

We all have a Promised Land. We all have a place we know exists that is outside of the current misery we're living in. We have a place (and position) we wish to be that is elevated beyond where we are now. Your Promised Land exists, but it requires you to become courageous as you pursue it.

One thing that helps me to be courageous is the fact that I focus on the future. I am very future-minded, which helps me to see beyond my current situation. Focusing so much on the future helps a ton because I don't get so caught up in the moment. I understand that I cannot get to my desired future destination without making a bold decision to help get me there now.

When I was in high school, I was on and off the cheerleading and pom-pom teams. At the end of my junior year, I tried out for the cheerleading team and made the varsity squad senior year. At the beginning of the season, I did not know how to tumble, but my heart was set on learning how to tumble. Though I had spent many years in tumbling and gymnastics, I had never learned how to fully run a tumbling pass that was worthy of a cheerleading performance.

So that summer I made it up in my mind that I was going to learn how to tumble. The cheerleading coach would bring in a tumbling instructor to help us with our form and technique. I took all the tumbling lessons seriously and was determined to learn how to do a round-off into a back-handspring before the summer was out.

So, every day at cheerleading practice, I would run passes across the floor. I gained enough courage to run an advanced pass with the help of someone assisting me for support. I worked my way up to successfully do a roundoff into a back-handspring with someone to spot me. I got to the point that everyone was so confident that I could do it alone and I didn't need help.

But when I went to tumble across the floor and there was nobody there to support me, I would always freak out. For some reason, I couldn't get to the back handspring without panicking and freezing up.

My support spotter would have to psych me out and go on the floor with me "just in case." One day, I tumbled across the floor and my support spotter moved his arm out the way without me knowing and I successfully completed the pass on my own.

I felt accomplished and overjoyed, but still nervous to do it alone. I got bold enough to do it again on my own without my support, but I crumbled. I wouldn't even run across the floor knowing that there was nobody there to spot me. The fear was all in my head. I was completely capable, but I was overthinking. I trusted my support spotter, but what I really needed to do was trust myself and my ability.

Sometimes we get so caught up thinking about the worst possible scenarios in situations that we forget our own ability. I had been training for this all summer long. I had been running laps to build my endurance. I had been lifting weights to build my strength, and I'd learned the technique and form to complete the pass successfully. I was ready, my body was ready, but my mind had to get into alignment.

Everyone else was watching me, cheering me on, and expecting me to get it right, but it wouldn't happen until my mind was ready. I kept trying.

One day I hyped myself up enough and told myself I could do it. Here's what was stopping me: I was afraid of falling on my head and I was afraid of getting hurt. I had to remind myself that I had done the tumbling pass before, and now all I had to do was believe I could do it, trust myself, and make the pass. I got the courage to try it alone.

I took an attempt at the pass. I started in one corner of the mat. I swiftly ran across the floor, placed my hands on the mat with perfect form to transition into my roundoff, my body glided through the air, and I did a back flip with my feet landing on the floor. I got so much height that my hands didn't even hit the ground for the back-handspring and instead I did a hands-free back flip.

I had just done something that was more difficult than what I was trying to do, and I did it seamlessly. I'll never forget that day. I was surprised at my achievement, and so was everyone else. That day, I learned to trust myself and my ability.

I had finally learned how to tumble in time for the cheerleading season. It was the vision I had that kept me determined to learn and never give up. That's my approach to most things. If I try my best and put my all into something, there's nothing that I cannot achieve. I just had to trust myself and get over my fear of the worst possible outcome.

It's the vision for my life and the impact that I'm called to have that push me to make bold decisions that don't always make sense. I see myself impacting the masses and living a life that inspires others to bet on themselves, trust God, and create a life they love. That vision is what keeps me motivated to never give up.

Remember I told you I was an overachiever? Well, that typically kicks in when I'm in pursuit of something I have my mind set on. I can be very dedicated and diligent in that regard. I believe every person deserves to trust themselves, their ability, and bet on themselves.

When I quit my job in corporate America, I had to make a decision to bet on myself. So, when it comes to the life I've always wanted and knew I deserved, I remind myself that I have to be both bold and courageous for the people that are following me into their own versions of the Promised Land.

## Building your Bold and Courageous Lifestyle

The first step to building a bold and courageous lifestyle is to have a very clear vision of your life and what your Promised Land looks like.

I believe that each of us has a God-given purpose that we are called to walk in. I believe we are specifically designed to execute that purpose during our lifetime. Every aspect of our character, personality, and makeup fit perfectly together into our purpose. God has given us gifts and talents that will help us walk in our purpose, but I also believe that He has given each of us passions and burdens that are unique to us.

Our passions and burdens make us who we are and can point us to the path to purpose more clearly.

Our passions are the things that ignite and illuminate us. Our passions can range from our talents to things that shape our life experiences. Some of these passions are learned and some of them have been in our spirits for years. One of my passions is to travel the world, and every time I travel, my life is illuminated even more.

Our burdens are the things about the world that we wish to change. I often say that you should examine the things that you cannot stand or simply hate to identify your burdens. Burdens are personal to you, and they may not matter as much to others as it matters to you. That's why it's your burden and not theirs.

For example, one of my life's burdens is for women who do not see their true value. I cannot stand to see brilliant, talented women and girls struggle with their confidence. As a woman who struggled to see myself as beautiful and capable for years, I hate to see other women struggle with the same thing. So, my burden in that area drives me to change that about the world. Again, my Promised Land is not about me, it's about the people I'm called to.

I believe that our personal Promised Land is the place where we are able to exist as our highest version of ourselves and answer the calling that is on our lives. It's the place where we can live in our purpose, unapologetically. Your purpose is intricately linked to your Promised Land. You, my friend, have to be bold and courageous to get there.

Let's explore what your Promised land looks like for you.

## Answer these questions to help you gain clarity about your Promised Land:

1. What's your bold and courageous vision?

2. What are your personal passions?

3. List your gifts and talents.

4. What are your personal burdens?

5. What do you wish you could change about the world?

6. What does the highest version of yourself look like?

7. What does your Promised Land look like?

8. Who does your Promised Land help?

# 2 *When You're Not Feeling Bold & Courageous*

One of the biggest enemies to your courage and boldness is fear. Let's talk about being fearless. I have noticed a trend in modern society that focuses on being fearless. It encourages us to be fearless, and while I think the original intent of the trend has positive origins, it has a major flaw. The concept of fearlessness creates an unrealistic expectation for ourselves. Fear is a natural human response. The problem with the concept of being fearless is that there really is no such thing as being truly fearless. Fear will always be present. Fear is inevitable.

Fear is an emotion that you have to face and be intentional about addressing. Fear shows up in so many different ways and can be camouflaged as many different things.

You'll hear me say this several times in this book: I do not claim to be fearless. I'm actually afraid quite often, but I don't allow fear to keep me stuck.

Instead of expecting yourself to be fearless, you should expect to be courageous. That is a more reasonable expectation of ourselves. Fear implies stagnation, while courage implies movement and advancement.

As humans, we typically applaud others for their courage, bravery, and strength. Those praises come from the understanding that there was an obstacle or mountain that had to be overcome. While fearlessness communicates that we as humans do not encounter fear in moments of bravery.

I don't know about you, but I'm tired of the world where we all pretend that our lives are picture perfect. I'm tired of the world of social media that tells us we have to present ourselves as if we never struggle. I try my best not to present my life that way online. I also commend those who show up with courage during tough seasons online. The goal is not to be fearless, rather, the goal is to move with purpose despite your fears. That, my friend, is courage.

Choosing courage requires a level of bravery, while choosing fear requires complacency. Here's what I mean. If you are faced with fear and decide to submit to it and back down, then you are complacent with your current situation. What you are communicating through your actions is that you would rather stay where you are and choose comfort over where you truly desire to be.

I'm here to tell you that fear is normal. It's completely okay to be afraid. It's something that we all experience. You don't have to hold yourself to the unrealistic expectation to be fearless. Since we've already made it clear that fear is going to show up, especially on your journey to the Promised Land, you just need to plan to face it.

When you face a fear, you will always have a choice. You will either choose courage or choose complacency. Just like when I was in high school during cheerleading practice, I had to learn that fear was mental.

Fear has two different aspects. On one hand, we have fears that are reasonable because they present an inherent danger. On the other hand, we have fears that are unreasonable because they are not based in fact and are ultimately based on assumptions.

During my time attempting tumbling passes in cheerleading, my fear was that I would hurt myself. That fear was reasonable because I was attempting something that could cause an injury. At the same time, that fear was unreasonable because I had received the training necessary to execute the tumbling pass without causing injury.

Oftentimes, when faced with fear, the things we deeply desire to do sit at the intersection of reasonable fear and unreasonable fear. That's also where our Promised Land exists. The outcome of what we do in the face of fear depends on our willingness to be uncomfortable.

When facing a fear, you have to ask yourself whether you want to choose the discomfort of staying where you are or the discomfort you'll encounter on the journey to where you want to be. I can promise you that both are going to cause some level of discomfort, but only one will leave you in a place of serious regret.

Fear is all about safety. As humans, we want to do what feels safe. None of us wants to willingly put our lives in danger.

We want to have a sense of safety and security in life, and it applies even when we make decisions.

The world that is familiar to us feels safe. As soon as you start to venture out into the unknown is when things get a little tricky. When you're in a place of unknown territory, everything is uncertain and taking steps with boldness and confidence can be terrifying.

When presented with fear, you will always have a choice. You either choose courage or you choose fear and complacency. Fear is our way of protecting ourselves from unknown, unforeseen dangers. When we choose fear, our minds convince ourselves that if we avoid the unknown territory then we will never have to experience the pain that it will inflict upon us. But if you choose fear, you will be both uncomfortable and discontent... always wondering "what if".

Courage requires discomfort. It requires that you get uncomfortable. We are often pushed into taking courageous steps toward our Promised Land when we get sick and tired of the discomfort that exists on the side of our fear.

I've always been an extremely analytical person. I think deeply and I typically think about every possible scenario in most situations. I'm the person that typically has a ton of questions because I want to know everything possible there is to know. I'm extremely calculated when it comes to my purpose and making decisions in life, in business, in relationships, and even with my finances.

When quitting my job in corporate America, I had so many fears. I was afraid that I would have to embarrassingly return to a similar job if my dreams of being a successful entrepreneur didn't work out. I was afraid that I would not be able to pay my bills or keep up the lifestyle I had grown comfortable with. I could not predict what was going to be the outcome of my decision, so I was afraid of the unknown.

By the time 2017 rolled around and I knew I wanted to quit my job, I had a little problem on my hands. I had grown extremely comfortable with the six-figure per year income I was earning. I was comfortable with getting paid twice a month and knowing that I had a consistent stream of income that I could trust and depend on.

I had just bought a house at the age of twenty-five one year prior. I had just gotten a new car that same year. I had responsibilities that depended on those consistent checks from my corporate job.

It was an interesting space to be in because I was completely fed up with my nine-to-five. I was drained because I was working late nights and early mornings. I was underappreciated and disrespected throughout many of my projects. I was miserable because there was no true work-life balance nor true rest. But somehow, I kept holding onto that life of misery because of a consistent check.

At the beginning of 2017 I went on a fast for mental clarity and to gain spiritual insight from God on my current season. After completing that fast, I was determined that it was the year I would quit my job. That fast gave me peace about my decision to quit my job that year. It helped me trust that I would have a successful, thriving career in entrepreneurship.

So, I picked a date: August 31, 2017. My plan was to work diligently, save up a minimum of $15,000, and quit my job on August 31st.

That year got crazy. During the first half of the year, my refrigerator and washing machine broke down and needed to be replaced, my basement completely flooded, and I had random, mandatory expenses that I was forced to pay. The little savings I had was depleted and instead of saving $15,000, I ended up with little-to-no savings at all.

Not only was my safety net of $15,000 non-existent, but I had no other source of income in my business. My blog "Epic Fab Girl" had launched the previous year but was not bringing in income. I had started driving Uber and Lyft on the weekends to add extra income to my savings account. The little money I was able to save was not going to be able to carry me through full-time entrepreneurship.

Quitting my job at that point simply did not make good financial sense. But staying on a job that kept me miserable and in poor mental health did not make good sense, either.

Those four-figure checks I was getting from my job were just like the support spotter during my cheerleading days. In the same way I trusted the spotter, I trusted the money way too much and I didn't trust myself to bring in that amount of money on my own.

To take it a step deeper, I trusted the money I was getting from my corporate job more than I trusted God's ability to provide. As a Christian entrepreneur, I have grown to understand that God is my source of provision. One of God's names is Jehovah Jireh, which means the Lord Provides. God is exactly who He says He is: a Provider.

Let's talk about how much we as humans trust money. Typically, if we don't have any money we find ourselves in complete misery. If we were to lose everything that we had in the bank and be completely wiped clean, many of us would feel an immensely heavy burden. It would be hard to get through the day without thinking about the fact that you have no money. It's almost as if money (or the lack thereof) tends to rule our minds and decisions. So much of our world is dependent on money. We need money for basic needs and luxuries, and because of it, our society has become so dependent on it.

Money doesn't just cover necessities and get us through life, money (and what it can buy) is a status symbol. Many people dream of a life of success that includes an influx of money. While there is nothing wrong with our need and desire for money, we must not trust money more than we trust the source of our money. I'm not talking about the source of our income (i.e., our jobs or careers), we must learn to trust the source of all provision: God.

One thing I love about God is that He is not just the Creator of the universe, but He is a father to each of us, individually. When we let God in, we can experience His fathering nature. A loving father gives of himself freely and provides based on not just our necessities but our desires.

Let me be clear that I do not believe that money is evil. I sincerely believe that money is good. It is the resource that we can use to walk in a greater level of purpose during this lifetime. Money is a good thing, and it's something that God desires to give you. Even the money that you get from a nine-to-five job comes from our ultimate source: God.

Psalm 84:11 NLT states, "For the LORD God is our sun and our shield. He gives us grace and glory. The LORD will withhold no good thing from those who do what is right."

That means that God, in all His goodness, will gladly give us good things (including money) because He is our ultimate source. I have been studying this concept for the past five to six years. In the Bible, Matthew 6:24 NIV states,

> "No one can serve two masters. Either you will hate the one and love the other, or you will be devoted to the one and despise the other. You cannot serve both God and money."

When we put our trust in money, that's when we transition from a healthy relationship with money into servanthood toward money. As a Christian, a part of our purpose is to worship and serve God. When we put our trust in money more than we trust God, we are exalting its power above the power of God. When we do this, we put ourselves in a place of worship and devotion toward money and remove God from His rightful place in our lives as the ultimate provider.

Even when done unintentionally, trusting money more than God causes us to create an idol out of money. That's dangerous territory to enter simply because it delays your entry into the Promised Land.

Every person that is called to enter their Promised Land will have to go through this test. You will be faced with the option to either trust money or trust God. If you find yourself consistently missing out on the Promised Land, you may have some idols to remove from your life.

I had to make the personal decision to trust God and His ability to provide for me so that I could have the courage to quit my job. The journey to quitting my job was scary though I knew God had promised me success in entrepreneurship. That was my Promised Land. However, on the way to the Promised Land, I was faced with fear. In the same way that God told Joshua to be strong and courageous when heading into the Promised Land, I took that assignment and message from God personally. But with that assignment came the understanding that God would be there every step of the way. I read this verse as if it was a personal command from God directly to me...

> "Have I not commanded you? Be strong and courageous. Do not be afraid; do not be discouraged, for the LORD your God will be with you wherever you go." (Joshua 1:9 NIV).

Trusting God personally gave me the courage to quit my job. This was one of those things that I could not trust in myself for. I had to, fully and completely, depend on God because I was entering into unknown territory. If it were up to me, I would have never quit my job when I did. I almost backed out and gave up.

Though I knew I had received a Master of Business Administration and I had run a successful hair extensions business in college, my training and my own strength was not enough for me to make that bold decision. I knew I needed God to make the scariest decision I've ever had to make.

The fact that God would be with me wherever I went was the thing that gave me courage to move forward. I whole-heartedly believe that God was the reason I quit.

Since quitting my job, I have become a successful, multiple-six-figure business owner. I personally know that I have entered my Promised Land, but it's only the beginning of it. There will always be another level of the Promised Land that we need to enter.

After Joshua in the Bible was instructed by God to enter the Promised Land, there were many battles he had to fight. The Promised Land is a place that represents victory and abundance, but it does not mean that it will be easy to enter it. In the same way, I believe that there are many struggles we may encounter as we enter and take over the Promised Land that God promises us. Fear will come up time and time again as you deal with different battles you will face in the Promised Land, but you must understand that God will be with you always.

We may have a Promised Land in our careers, families, health, and so many different areas of our lives. On the journey to the promise, I can assure you that fear will be there, but so will God. It's okay to be afraid, but it's how you respond to fear that helps you enter and thrive in the Promised Land.

I've personally experienced fear at so many moments in my life, and I've had to learn how to respond to them. Every time I face a new area of fear, I'm able to remember the last time I was afraid and overcame it. Most times I realize that there was no real reason for me to be afraid to begin with, but that helps me have a better perspective on how to respond to future fears that may come up. I've also learned that the more that I do scary things, the more courageous I become. Fear tends to leave you when you do scary things. With every step you take you become more courageous, and you must make a conscious decision of choosing courage over fear.

## Take some time to answer these prompts to help you identify moments in your life where you haven't felt bold and courageous.

1. When you're afraid, what is your typical response?

2. What are you most afraid of?

3. Identify the moments in your life when you experienced fear and overcame it.

4. What courageous decisions have you made in the past?

5. In what ways can you be more courageous in the future?

6. What reasonable fears have you experienced in your life?

7. What unreasonable fears have you experienced in life?

# 3 *Bold & Courageous Reflections*

To become a bold and courageous authority, one must courageously take a look within to explore the pain of your past. This chapter is dedicated to identifying areas in your life that have been attacking your confidence. You may want to rush through this, but I challenge you to take your time. You may want to jump to figuring out solutions to dealing with what comes up, but this chapter is not about that. This chapter is about reflecting, laying it all out, and bringing what you discover out of hiding.

Now that we know fear is perfectly normal, you have to do a little bit of digging to figure out the source of the unreasonable fears that arise in your life. Those unreasonable fears are the fears that hold you back from entering the Promised Land.

We must do work to figure out what has shaped us into the person we are today. We have to examine what has impacted our world view and outlook on life. It's important to gain an understanding of how we view ourselves and how that has been shaped over time. Let's get to it!

After I left the "gifted" school on Chicago's south side in fourth grade, my parents transferred me to a new school in Chicago's south suburbs. It was a whole new world if you ask me. I could finally escape my past life and avoid being called "Ms. Piggy" at last! Life seemed a lot more pleasant from the start, but shortly after transitioning to this new school the teasing picked up again. This time I was teased for my size and my shape much more frequently.

I can find humor in it now because Brazilian Butt Lifts are a trend, but in the fourth grade I was teased about my big butt. My playground besties thought it would be humorous to give me the nickname "Bubble Butt". I'd get on the school bus to go home and there was a consistent comment about my butt on the daily. I continued to be teased about my size, and I had become convinced that something was wrong with me the way I existed.

Going from "Ms. Piggy" to "Bubble Butt" was not the most graceful entry into a new school. Not only did I struggle with being teased at school, I would go home to my siblings who would light me up with insults.

My parents raised four kids in the same house, and most of the time it was chaotic. Tons of yelling and screaming. But at times things were peaceful, usually when we could all agree on what to watch on TV.

My siblings were just plain old mean to me. The major insult they said to me growing up was that I was fat, and most of the time my parents were too occupied with adult responsibilities to notice the insults and protect me from them. My two older siblings would be mean and by the time my younger brother was old enough to speak, they found a way to have him gang up on me, too.

The most peace I got as a kid was from being alone. So, when I was at home, I spent a ton of time alone and focused on my hobbies or school work.

It didn't make it any better that I was the high performer of the family. I was the kid who tested into the "gifted" program that made it possible for my siblings to attend Beasley. I was the kid who got straight A's all throughout elementary and junior high school. My parents ate that up. They were ridiculously proud of my achievements, and they made it known in the house — and pretty much everywhere else, for that matter.

That added more fuel to my siblings' fire. That turned into them resenting me because I was the over-achiever and got so much praise from my parents. I never really got in trouble for much of anything (except for liking boys at a super young age). My siblings dubbed me the "Golden Child" and they hated me for it. They'd call my parents out for treating me differently, and my parents would deny it. But we all knew my parents treated me differently because I behaved differently.

My parents focused so much on my achievements that my needs in the areas of mental wellness and self-acceptance were overlooked. My parents didn't really have the opportunity to affirm me because of this oversight. They didn't have the chance to properly address the negative self-image I had been developing because my achievements overshadowed it.

As an adult I learned that my parents sent one of my siblings to counseling and I always wondered why my needs had been overlooked. I definitely needed counseling, too. My needs were overlooked simply because my parents were so focused on my achievements and talents that they didn't notice the silent and subtle struggles I was dealing with. It was a world of smoke and mirrors. From the outside looking in, I was the "perfect child," but I was battling internally with my existence.

The lack of affirmation from my parents and the hatred I experienced from my siblings and peers drove me to a place of self-hatred. It was almost as if while the world was amplifying my achievements, I was internally amplifying all the negativity the world had spewed my way. My response as a kid was to throw myself into my achievements.

I suffered in silence for so many years. By junior high school, I compared myself to other little girls wondering why my body was different. I wondered why I couldn't just be skinny like the other kids, and I promised myself that I would never get truly "fat" one day. The thought of not being fat ruled so much of my thought life. I would overly consider what I would eat, I was afraid to eat in front of others for fear of being teased about what or how I ate, and I even began to suffer from bulimia.

My decisions at the time were all driven by wanting to avoid that painful feeling of being teased, talked about, or mistreated. I never wanted anyone to have that type of power over me, so I tried to control it by causing harm to my body.

I'll never forget one year in junior high school; I was rapidly losing weight and one of the administrators pulled me aside. She was the type of woman with an old soul who felt like she could be the most nurturing grandma but also hip enough to want to hang around all the time. She gave the best hugs. When she pulled me into a room privately, she looked me in my face and said, "Baby you are beautiful, don't let anybody else tell you anything different. You do not need to change yourself nor your body to be beautiful. You are beautiful just as you are." She hugged me tight, and I rushed to my next class.

I felt like she knew my secret. I felt like she could see what nobody else had seen for so long because they were so focused on my achievements. She could see that I struggled with seeing myself as beautiful and I was doing whatever I knew how just to avoid the pain of being teased.

Though I did not always consciously recognize it, I developed a deep fear of what people had to say about me. I feared others' negative words about me, so in turn I wanted to be friends with everyone so that I would never experience feelings of rejection. I had a deep desire to be accepted because I felt like that was the only way to truly avoid having people talk bad about me.

Though I wanted to be accepted by everyone, I still hated being the center of attention. I could not stand when people focused their eyes and attention on me (even if it was good attention) because it gave me anxiety. In the back of my head, I'd always wonder what negative things they'd be saying (or thinking) about me.

When you experience constant negativity from the people closest to you for so long, you build up several defense mechanisms and trauma responses. My trauma response was to protect myself at all costs and avoid any type of spotlight.

I never cared about having the spotlight — I never wanted it. It freaked me out because it would literally shine a light on me — good and bad. Attention would expose all aspects of me, especially the aspects I didn't really like about myself to begin with. I didn't want others to see the things that I had personally grown to hate, either. I hated my nose. I hated my weight. I hated that I could never find jeans that properly fit my big butt.

Remember, I told you I was popular by accident, right? Coming into my freshman year of high school, I just wanted to know as many people as possible. The goal was (in the back of my mind) to be likable by everyone. If I could be friends with everyone I met, there would never be anything negative for them to say about me, right? That's what I thought, at least.

I spent the summer before high school playing sports which meant I slimmed down and lost my "baby fat". Any remnant of chubbiness from puberty was gone. I was a whole new girl on the outside, but I was still that damaged little girl on the inside. I was still convinced that I was fat, though I stood 4'11.5 inches tall and weighed 135 pounds, with a big butt. In comparison to the other girls, I was still convinced that I was too big.

So, I was extremely surprised when I got so many compliments for being pretty. I was shook when I got attention from even the cutest guys in school. I went from being teased about my big butt to being praised for it. I started to hear from so many people that they thought I was pretty, and I caught wind that I was considered one of the prettiest girls in my class.

Me? Pretty?! I remember wondering what it was that they saw. I was literally so confused, and it didn't make sense to me. I literally thought I was ugly because of the negative words from my peers in the fourth grade. I seriously thought I was fat and that my nose looked like a pig's snout. But, since I kept getting compliments that I was pretty in high school, I started to accept it.

I accepted that people thought I was pretty, but internally, I truly never really felt pretty or beautiful. I just now knew that the world considered me a pretty girl.

Freshman year at Homewood-Flossmoor High School was a great year, but then I also started to see how everybody wasn't really my friend. I was nominated for homecoming court for the freshman class alongside three of my closest friends. During the period between final nominations and the big reveal, rumors began to spread like wildfire within some pockets of the school.

I remember one day a girl came up to me in the hallway and said that she heard a rumor that I said I was going to win homecoming court over the rest of my friends because I was light skinned. I completely froze. Those words never left my mouth, but I had to quickly defend myself. I said, "I would never say something like that. All my friends are pretty." I went on to explain why I thought each of the other girls deserved the crown and how we all had an equal shot.

Whew... the drama. I remember feeling like I had been stabbed in the chest from a false accusation about something I had never said. I was annoyed because I already hated how there was such a divide in the black community about beauty amongst skin tones. I was so annoyed with the thought that people were thinking I was arrogant or thought I was better than others because of how I looked.

Now you know, since you're reading this book, that I didn't even see myself as beautiful, so I did not think I had a chance at winning. I never thought that I'd be the one who was chosen. I wondered where the heck she got that lie from and who thought it was a good idea to make up something so terrible about me. I already hated attention, but I surely did not like this type of negative attention.

I brushed it off and went through the rest of the week still anxious to learn who was going to win.

My high school was the type where kids were not always the nicest. The upperclassmen wouldn't always be nice to the freshmen. They would even hurl pennies at some freshmen to torture them since they were newbies. Now that I think about it, it was a rough place simply because of the social experience, at times. I'd learn later that reputation was everything in the hallways of that school.

The day of the homecoming pep rally finally arrived. When it was time to announce the freshman class winners, I sat there anxiously waiting to hear who would win. Though I did not think I would win, I wanted to win simply for the sake of winning. Because of my family's constant praise of my accomplishments, I had grown addicted to achievement and I hated losing.

With the entire student body of over 4,000 students watching and waiting, they announced… This year's freshman homecoming court winner is Candace Armour.

The crowd flooded with a mixture of excitement and boos. I had no idea how to respond. I was excited to win, but I was completely caught off guard with the negative response of the crowd. I wondered if the boos from the crowd were just because I was a freshman or if it was because of the negative rumors.

For a girl who was already traumatized by the negative words of her siblings and peers growing up, this was my worst nightmare: public humiliation. Somehow, I didn't crack or shed a tear even though inside I wanted to burst. I just clung tightly onto my escort's arm and did my best to make it across the floor and back without falling. It was literally the worst — all eyes on me, and I hated every moment of it.

Yet again, my achievements were causing me pain in a similar way it did with my siblings. So that was the beginning of me consciously and consistently choosing to dim my light to make others feel comfortable with my existence. I'd later learn to stop dimming my light, but it took lots of intentionality for me to show up in my brilliance without concern of what others would have to say or think about it.

# 3.1 *Reflecting on Your Biggest Fears*

Walking in our God-given authority requires us to make the courageous decision to reflect within ourselves and take note of the things that have made us develop unreasonable fears. Let's get into the most common types of fear you will encounter on the journey to the Promised Land:

## Fear of what people will say

Fear of what others have to say about you is rooted in the fear of being rejected. Our innate desire to be accepted by others is not bad, it's normal. Acceptance by others makes us feel safe, and our desire for safety is normal. However, shifting to be accepted, though commonly practiced, is not normal.

True acceptance from others comes when you're able to fully be your true self and be accepted that way. The problem comes in when we shift ourselves to make ourselves more palatable and acceptable to others. Because of fear, many of us have been conditioned to shift ourselves, our nature, our existence, our mannerisms, and even our words to be more easily digestible and accepted by others.

Living in fear of what others have to say is extremely damaging. We are never truly able to be the truest version of ourselves, and it's almost like you're living a double life. You'll have two versions of reality: the real you and the version of you that you present to the world.

Let's face it. It's not easy to present your true self to the world when you've encountered so much hurt and pain. The world can be mean, vicious, backbiting, and (especially in the landscape of social media) judgmental.

The fear of what others have to say about you becomes an enemy to your purpose if you continue to submit to it. Your purpose is linked to your Promised Land. Your purpose will never come alive if you remain fearful of what others have to say about you.

Humans have talked about others for generations — ever since the beginning of time. We all know that both oral storytelling and folklore were some of the major ways that information was shared throughout generations. It's because stories are easily shareable and because humans love to talk. Talking is how people connect with others, and while sometimes what people say may not have a negative motive, it can have both positive and negative effects on us and our world view.

People will talk about you when you're doing well. People will talk about you when you're doing not-so-well. People will talk about you regardless, so just do what you were called to do anyway.

One of the things that has helped me overcome the fear of what others think or say about me is this: I don't give energy to it. I consciously free myself from the opinions of others. How do I do this? I ask myself this one question: What's the worst that could happen?

Oftentimes when we fear what others think or say, we are imagining an exaggerated negative outcome that will leave us miserable. I'm kind of a pro at thinking through the most random potential outcomes and scenarios. I can tell you that it's draining to dwell on a world of "what ifs". However, I'm going to teach you how to use those worst possible outcome scenarios to fuel your forward movement.

To free myself from others' opinions, I think through what the worst possible outcome could possibly be. I then take those scenarios and identify what I'm really, truly afraid of. To deal with those thoughts of fear, I have to be self-aware and intentionally address and dismantle them.

Let's use a personal example from my life. When I was originally planning my brand Epic Fab Girl's first ever Go-Getter Conference for women entrepreneurs, I was planning the event with a limited budget. I had just quit my job in corporate America, and I had no idea what I was doing, but I wanted to focus on hosting this event to empower women. I made a list of a few of the biggest names I knew of at the time and began reaching out to those women to speak.

Initially, every keynote speaker I pitched to speak at the conference ignored my email. I was stumped trying to figure out who I could get to speak at my conference. The only other thing I knew to do was ask other impactful women in my current network who I had some sort of relationship with, but I was scared.

At first, I didn't reach out because I was convinced that their speaking rates were too high and I wouldn't be able to afford them. Once I talked myself into reaching out, one of the speakers responded and requested that I share how much we could pay her. The problem was I wasn't quite sure what to offer her. I was nervous that if I offered something too low that she'd be insulted by my request, and I did not want that to negatively affect her view of me or my brand. I put a random number that I thought was fair and she gracefully accepted the offer. Whew… I went from sweating bullets to complete relief.

I was afraid to reach out to that keynote speaker simply because I was afraid of what she would think about me. I was afraid that if she didn't like my offer, she would reject it and tell her friends and peers that I insulted her with such a low offer. I was using fear to protect myself from the potential of damaging my reputation…the same way my reputation had been damaged at several points in high school. However, I had to ask myself what's the worst that could really happen? The only reasonable answer was she would say "no". But I was afraid that the "no" I would get would be one that was painful. I could deal with "no" but I didn't like the thought of hearing "no" with an additional negative response on the back end of it.

In all my time hosting events over the past six years, I have only received ONE negative response to a proposal to speak. It read:

> "It's very disheartening to me that you'd reach out with an unpaid speaking opportunity while there seems to be different messaging on your social media platform and marketing: helping women scale to 6-figures on social and getting paid what we're worth. This commission-based opportunity is not a good use of my time and platform. There seems to be a disconnect here and respectfully, I will have to decline."

The audacity. When I read that email, it initially stung because I personally knew this woman and she had previously spoken at a past event of ours. I had to sit on it for a while and figure out how to respond without the need to defend myself or apologizing… and without matching her negative energy. That little girl from Beasley in me wanted to fight to defend herself, but as a courageous woman of influence, I could not. And that's just not how I operate anyways. All I could think of was Michelle Obama's graceful statement: "When they go low, we go high."

Here's the conclusion I came to: The woman was right; spending her time in front of a positive group of Christian women entrepreneurs wasn't a good use of her time. And even better, she helped weed herself out from the positive culture and community I worked so hard to create. Her response taught me two major things: (1) any woman who I'd want to grace the stage at any of our events would never respond negatively or disrespectfully, and (2) every battle is not yours to fight.

Though I felt her response to me was disrespectful and was an attempt to challenge my character and values, I responded to her with a simple: "Thank you so much. I hope you enjoy the rest of your week."

The old me would have been quick to apologize to her for offending her, but I could not bring myself to do it. Why? There was nothing to apologize to her for.

My brand, Epic Fab Girl, which had limited resources, was trying something new to generate revenue for our business and also pay our speakers on the back end. This business is completely separate from my personal brand, Candace Junée, and also has completely separate budgets and profit models. We were hosting a virtual experience and trying the option of offering our speakers affiliate commissions for the first time. This was a business decision I made with my team, and it was not a personal matter.

I initially wanted to respond to her saying, "This wasn't meant to offend you" or "I didn't mean to communicate the wrong message," but I had to realize that nothing more needed to be said to defend myself. I had pitched several other speakers with the same proposal, and they all accepted and a few politely and respectfully declined. It simply was not a good fit for her, and I didn't need to apologize for asking.

Imagining the worst in this situation, I knew there was a possibility she could choose to speak negatively about me and my brand to others. But, I had to be okay with the fact that she could do that, and if she did, it would not be a negative reflection on me and my brand.

It takes courage not to try to defend yourself when the thing you fear actually creates a negative scenario for you. It takes courage to treat someone with respect when you've felt disrespected.

So, like I said before, when you're faced with fear of what people think, you have to ask yourself what's the worst that could happen. Most times the outcome will be in your favor. Even if you end up in a sucky situation, you'll still be able to grow from it. It's a win-win if you ask me.

When you're faced with fear, ask yourself these three questions:

1. What am I really afraid of?
2. Why am I so afraid of that outcome?
3. What's the worst that could happen?

But don't just sit there, think it through! Once you come up with a response, you'll be able to get to the bottom of what you're really afraid of and why.

Once you have the response for, "What's the worst that could happen?"... ask yourself "Andddd?" Your response should be: "even if that does happen, it's not the end of the world. I am still a brilliant human regardless."

You can always overcome the worst thing that could happen. People are going to talk, regardless. You are going to be phenomenal, regardless.

● ● ●

Another one of the most common types of fear you will encounter on the journey to the Promised Land is:

# Fear of rejection

The fear of rejection is so trickyyyyyy! It loves to camouflage itself as other things, so you have to get good at pointing it out and recognizing it quickly. The fear of rejection is often at the root of most unreasonable fears. We are afraid of being rejected by people and opportunities. And we even fear our success for fear of rejection on a larger platform and scale.

Fear of rejection causes so many people to never try. It likes to camouflage itself as other things like procrastination, for example. Let's say you have to submit an important presentation to a potential business investor. You know the meeting is in two weeks, but you wait until the night before to do the work because "you don't know what to put in it". What's really happening is that you have convinced yourself that this business investor is going to reject your ideas and pick you apart as a result. You're afraid of being rejected. You imagine yourself deteriorating on the inside while the investor points out the flaws in your vision and business structure. So instead of giving your presentation everything you have, you throw it together the night before because you were "so overwhelmed" with the thought of putting it together. In reality, you played yourself because you were playing scared. You stepped onto the slippery slope of self-sabotage.

## The fear of rejection camouflaged as self-sabotage

Let's say you come across a business coach that you believe is going to help you get to the next level. They have the results to prove that they're an expert and they've helped hundreds of others achieve the same results you desire to get. So, you say "yes" to the program. You're excited to get started; you sign a contract that states the program is non-refundable and you invest the $5,000 to enroll in the program.

Once you pay your fee, you have one session with your coach and then you start to feel like the information won't work for you. You then start to wonder if what you learned will really work for you. You give it a couple of days and you send an email to your coach to ask for a refund despite the no refund policy. You're playing the dangerous game of self-sabotage because you're afraid of the world rejecting you when you launch out with your new business ideas after coaching.

You're afraid to fail. You're afraid that you, specifically, won't be good enough for the program to work for you. You're convinced that it works for other people, but you're not convinced that it will work for you. You ruin all chances of success using those methods because you won't even attempt to put what you learned into practice. You, my friend, are afraid of failure.

## The fear of rejection camouflaged as fear of failure

Let's say you get an opportunity to apply for your dream job. Several people send you the job application because they think you're a perfect match for the role and they're even willing to be listed as references. The job is such an incredible position, and, though you have the experience and the resume to back it, you are nervous about applying for the job.

You would love to have the position because it is actually a perfect fit for you. You're so excited and nervous about it.

You're so nervous that you talk yourself out of applying for the role. You've convinced yourself that though you have experience, they won't pick you. You are afraid of failure, but ultimately, you're afraid of being rejected. You're afraid of having to deal with the pain of that rejection. You dread having to tell the others who recommended you for the role that you didn't get it.

You are afraid of your reputation being negatively affected because you want the world to view you as perfect, and this will make them view you differently. Your excessive attention to detail isn't just about your skill and your talent, but rather it's your fear of rejection camouflaged as perfectionism.

### Fear of rejection camouflaged as: perfectionism

Don't hate me for this, but we have to do some deep digging. Perfectionism doesn't always happen because we like to see things "perfect". It doesn't necessarily delight our souls to see things perfectly in their place: our work, our lives, ourselves included. The true delight is in the fact that others view us as perfect; it feeds our ego.

When we try to be perfect, we are trying our best to avoid rejection from the world. We are afraid of others being critical of us, which means that their criticism will indicate that we are not good enough. We never want to feel that way, so we do everything we can to make sure things are perfect. We throw ourselves so deeply into our work because it is a reflection of us.

Let's say you have a business idea you want to launch. You've had this idea for over ten years, and you've even seen some people launch a similar idea. You know the business has a proven track record for success, but you're afraid to put the business out there. You've been working on business plans behind the scenes for the past three years; you've created an Instagram handle, and you even set up a website. But the world doesn't know about it yet because you want to launch your business at the perfect moment when everything is just as perfect as you like it.

The reality is that you may never launch your business because you are trying so hard to be perfect. You're afraid that your idea and your business won't be accepted by others. Your perfectionism is really rooted in your deep desire to be accepted, and it's holding you back from walking into your Promised Land. You do your best to control how the world views you, so you try to hold yourself to the unrealistic expectation of perfection.

The reality is your perfectionism is rooted in your desire to control the way the world views you... because you're afraid of being rejected.

### Fear of rejection camouflaged as control

I'm a recovering control freak. I like to control things to keep them as perfect as possible. But perfection isn't possible, so I have been learning to let go of the things I cannot control. Oftentimes we try to control outcomes simply because we want things to turn out perfect.

For those recovering control freaks, like me, we leave little room for allowing ourselves and others to make mistakes because we expect an unrealistic expectation of perfection. We are fearful that if we do not control things, they will completely fall apart and be a poor reflection of ourselves. Our control is a defense mechanism to protect ourselves against our biggest fears.

There are various degrees of control, but the less controlling you are, the better of an asset you are to any environment you enter. Please don't feel bad about yourself if you struggle with being controlling. You should feel empowered now that you can recognize what's happening and release yourself from the fear of rejection so that you don't have to focus so much on controlling what you cannot control.

I have now become the person that courageously lets things go. I am at peace with outcomes that I cannot control, and I trust that all things will eventually settle. Making the decision to do that has brought so much peace in my life and removes so much stress from my life.

● ● ●

As we get closer to the Promised Land, there will always be more fears we have to dismantle. This next fear is quite delicate and close to our hearts:

## Fear of being hurt

When I was a kid, growing up in my family was chaotic. My mom was loving and attentive to detail, but always found a way to correct us when she thought we were wrong. My dad was a hard worker; he was always busy with work or relaxing after work.

My dad had two sides to him: one that was loving, sensitive, and hilarious, and the other that was unpredictable and volatile. My father's unpredictable nature made the entire family have to tiptoe around him to keep him pleased. We did our best to make sure not to do anything to make him upset for fear that he would explode into anger.

There were times when my father was physically abusive to my mom. There were even times when my dad would get so angry that he'd punch a wall or a door, leaving a hole behind. Instead of repairing the walls and doors around the house, a mirror or a picture would be placed on top of the wall to cover up what had been done. For years, this was a family secret that nobody knew of. This built a culture of secrecy around the home.

I witnessed my parents fight physically when I was young. As I got older, my parents would argue, and there were often arguments that would last for days or weeks and disrupt any peace there was in the home.

My siblings and I hated getting in trouble and having to face my dad after he found out. If at all possible, we wanted to avoid having my dad find out about any trouble at all costs. Even when we wanted something (like a new bike or to sleep over at a friend's house), my mom would tell us to ask our dad. We hated having to ask my dad for permission to do anything because we almost always knew it was going to be a "no".

As an adult, I've realized the impact of my childhood on my approach to life. I would be afraid to deal with conflict and even afraid to ask others simple questions or favors for fear of them telling me "No". I subconsciously developed this fear of making other people angry, so I held parts of myself back just to make myself more palatable for others. I literally walked on eggshells just to avoid volatile responses from others. I did that because I developed a fear of being hurt.

When you develop a fear of being hurt, your only goal is to protect yourself at any cost. You may not even be consciously aware that you've built up walls of self-protection against intruders to your peace. The problem with trying to defend yourself from being hurt is that everyone isn't going to treat you like the person that hurt you.

Sometimes we don't speak up or confront a situation because we are afraid of being hurt. Sometimes we don't say what we truly want to say for fear of being hurt. All are signs that you need to heal from your past and step into the freedom that it brings.

It takes courage to examine your past and look within to identify those moments that caused you pain in the past. It's important to recognize that everybody is not going to hurt you like those who have hurt you in the past. Establishing this belief is important in your Promised Land so that you can eventually build healthy relationships that allow you to thrive and be authentically you.

● ● ●

The Promised Land is the place where we thrive and experience the best success in life, but we can't get to the land of milk and honey if we are afraid of success itself.

# Fear of success

When we're talking about the Promised Land, it's the land where we exist as the highest version of ourselves. We cannot discuss the Promised Land without bringing up the topic of success. Fear of success is one of the major hindrances to our purpose and ability to thrive in the Promised Land.

When dealing with the fear of success, we are afraid that if we get to a place of success, we won't be able to handle it. We're afraid that we won't be able to maintain success, and we're afraid that all eyes on us will cause us to crumble under the pressure.

The fear of success will have you saying "no" to amazing opportunities that would be great for you. It'll have you procrastinating and never launching out. It'll have you playing safe and avoiding taking risks. Here's the thing about the journey to the Promised Land: You will have to take risks to get there. You cannot be so calculated that you are afraid to take risks that will get you closer to your success.

Taking risks can be scary, especially if you're an analytical person like me. If you're anything like me, you like to take risks that "make sense". It's quite laughable when you think about the concept of attempting to take a risk that makes sense.

Fear of success is often rooted in the fear of rejection, too. We're often afraid of exposing our true selves to the world and that they won't like it. We're afraid that if we accomplish something praiseworthy that we will not be able to live up to the hype.

The truth is your success won't be detrimental to your existence. There may be painful moments while existing in the space of success, but that doesn't mean you should let that fear stop you. In life we are bound to experience pain in some sort of way, but it's not your job to worry about it now.

It's natural and normal to fail on your way to your Promised Land. A momentary failure is not a forever failure. There is no failure that you cannot bounce back from, so you have to get comfortable with it and release yourself from the fear of failure.

## Fear of Failure

The fear of failure can have you paralyzed. When we're talking about your Promised Land, there is a journey required to get you there. It requires forward movement, not paralysis. Oftentimes, we are afraid of letting ourselves or others down. We are afraid of failing and the possibility of failure negatively impacting our well-being and reputation.

The fear of failure can often show up and hinder you from taking action if you let it stop you. It can look like this: you're afraid that things won't work out right when you try so you don't try. You say things like, "I don't want to look stupid," but in reality, you're afraid of failing in front of others. There's definitely fear of rejection hidden in there, too.

If you have a history of experiencing verbal abuse, teasing, or bullying, fear can be a defense mechanism against pain for you. For those who have been called "dumb" or "stupid" by others, they often fear failing for fear of looking dumb or stupid in others' eyes or even their own eyes.

Sometimes the fear of failure can be camouflaged as the desire to get a second opinion from others on everything. If you depend so much on others' opinions about you, your work, what you wear, how you style your hair, etc., it may be a sign that you want approval from someone who feels "safe" so that you don't have to fail more visibly in front of others. As you become better at dealing with the fear of failure, you may take steps forward and find yourself with a new problem to deal with: the fear of making mistakes.

● ● ●

We all get things wrong sometimes. This next fear often hinders you from taking action on the journey to and while existing in your Promised Land:

## Fear of Making Mistakes

The fear of making mistakes is a dressed-up version of the fear of failure or perfectionism. Oftentimes when you fear failure, you don't end up taking the leap to take any risky action. However, the fear of making mistakes typically shows up on the journey right after you've made a courageous decision. Or right before you're getting ready to make a decision that could change your life forever.

I've learned that the fear of making mistakes can often come from a fear of being judged by others or fear of not being able to live up to others' expectations.

There are some people who fear relationships, commitment, and even marriage simply because they're afraid of getting things wrong and making mistakes. People who struggle with this would rather not attempt a committed relationship for fear that they are not going to be able to live up to the expectations of that relationship. It has absolutely nothing to do with the other person and everything to do with the individual's fear of not being good enough and fear of failing. Their internal insecurities are amplified and cause them to avoid the relationship at any cost — or even worse, sabotage a relationship.

As someone who's choosing to walk in your God-given authority, you will have to own the fact that there will be mistakes made along the journey. Embrace the fact that you will not be perfect and that some of your failures and mistakes will be visible to others, some on a larger scale than others. However, never allow the fear of making mistakes stop you from showing up as your true, most authentic self.

• • •

This next fear is one that may cause you to attempt to exist as another version of yourself that is not the highest version of yourself. Remember that your Promised Land needs the highest version of yourself, so identifying this next fear will help you see how you may have shifted yourself based on your environment.

# Fear of Abandonment

The fear of abandonment can be a tricky little devil. Fear of abandonment stems from us taking the blame for others abandoning or neglecting us. We figure we must have been able to do something different to change the outcome of the situation, so in turn we begin to tiptoe with our decisions to avoid the pain of someone else walking out.

In situations like this, you begin to make calculated decisions that are not what you would have intrinsically desired to make. You shift your behaviors to make them more palatable for others so that you don't push them away.

Sometimes our fears of being left alone or having someone completely walk away from us drives our inability to be as bold and courageous as we would like to be. When you have experienced someone like a parent or a romantic partner walk away from you, abandon you, or be completely absent or neglectful, you likely struggle with some form of abandonment issues.

When I was a child, my parents would sometimes argue, and it would escalate to the point where my father would pack his bags and threaten to leave. There was always this impending threat that he would leave and completely walk away from my mom and his children. I can recount several times when my father would leave and be gone for days or weeks because he was arguing with my mom.

As a child, it made me wonder what my mom did or what we did to make my dad so upset to want to leave us. It must have been something we did wrong, right? I remember one time my dad sat at the bottom of the stairs with his bags packed and I cried and pleaded with him telling him, "Please don't go, daddy!" Imagine me in full-blown tears expecting my actions to convince my dad to stay. That little girl who desperately wanted her dad to stay home was let down because her father continued to leave and go absent for days and weeks at a time.

On this journey to the Promised Land, you have to be honest with yourself about the areas where abandonment and neglect may have reared their ugly heads and impacted how you make decisions. When faced with making decisions, you have to be careful not to be swayed by your own fears of being neglected or abandoned.

• • •

The next fear we will cover can come up often when we have experienced pain in our childhood or in relationships that involved inconsistent people. Now we are going to deal with the fear that shifts our expectations: the fear of being let down.

## Fear of being let down

Depending on other people is something you have to do as you walk in your God-given authority. A person who walks in authority is not on an island, rather they must interact with and depend on others to thrive in the fullness of their potential.

One of the biggest things that will stop you from being able to truly depend on others is the fear of being let down or disappointed. Operating from that place will hinder your success and your ability to accelerate quickly.

Here are a few examples of how the fear of being let down can show up in your life:

- You're afraid to give work to others for fear it won't meet your standards
- You micromanage others' projects, tasks, and responsibilities
- You take on too much responsibility
- Your default is to expect the worst-case scenario in a situation instead of expecting the best
- You don't expect the best for your future

If you've dealt with consistently being let down in the past, you may develop an intense fear of being let down or expect to be let down. It's possible that being let down in the past has caused you embarrassment or frustration so you may be afraid of depending on others.

The fear of being let down can develop from experiences like empty promises from a parent or caregiver or broken promises from a friend or romantic partner. We have all been let down at some point in our lives, but when it becomes consistent and repetitive, it can become traumatic.

A sign that you may be dealing with the fear of being let down is that you don't ask for what you really want. You may settle or ask for less than what you really desire because you're afraid of being let down. Or in even worse circumstances, you may not ask for anything at all because you do not want to be let down. In these situations, you just say, "forget about it".

Another sign that you may be dealing with the fear of being let down is that you don't expect anything or much from others. You expect the least. You don't expect for people to show up and do their part. This unhealthy cycle of dysfunction causes you to prepare yourself to be let down for others, so you make decisions from that perspective.

When you make decisions based on the fear of being let down, what you're really communicating to the world is that you don't really trust other people. Once you recognize that you fear being let down, you must eventually do the work to recover and move forward intentionally.

● ● ●

Oftentimes the fear of being let down leads to the fear of trusting other people. On your journey to and through the Promised Land, you must be able to trust others to have success and a healthy, fruitful life. Let's jump into the fear of trusting others.

## Fear of trusting other people

Trust is essential in healthy relationships with other people. Whether you need to trust them to do a task, trust them to have your back, trust them to keep a private matter confidential, or trust them with a vulnerable moment, trust is an important aspect of the journey into the Promised Land.

In high school, I became unexpectedly popular and had gained lots of "friends" from intentionally getting to know people. After I was crowned winner of homecoming court freshman year, I started to notice a lot of changes in my group of friends and how they responded to me.

I was typically the girl who minded my business, got good grades, and was a part of many extracurricular activities. But I was always very interested in boys. During freshman year, I had a major love interest and experienced "falling in love" with my first boyfriend at age fourteen. Of course, I got in trouble with my parents because I was not allowed to have a boyfriend until senior year, but I completely disregarded everything they had to say. I'd sneak around just so I could do whatever I wanted because my parents were so strict. Shortly after my first "serious" boyfriend and I broke up, I was interested in different guys and got attention from several different guys. That season of life slowly, but surely, turned into a slippery slope of promiscuity.

I'd start to get to know a guy and go through the talking or butterfly stages of getting to know each other. The relationship (or 'situationship') would usually progress to the point where eventually we would have some sort of sexual experience. After a while, I started to notice that after intimate sexual experiences, some guys would completely ghost me or break up with me. These were guys who told me they loved me. These were guys who said whatever it took to get what they wanted from me. There was even one guy who I never had sex with who lied and told others he had sex with me. I experienced heartbreak but it also became damaging to my self-worth.

I was one of the first girls in my friend group to lose her virginity. I'd tell my closest girlfriends secrets about my sexual experiences and even who I was crushing on at the time.

After a while, I decided I wasn't into the guys who were super popular. I'd be attracted to intellect or personality, so I'd end up dating guys that others weren't really that interested in nor paying much attention to. Junior year rolled around, and I started dating this one guy that not many people knew. He was smart, attractive, and pretty shy. He wasn't the type to hang out with the popular kids, but after we dated, most kids in the school knew his name and he even got connected with people in my friend group. We dated exclusively for a little while and got to know each other well. It felt like we were good for each other, and it felt like things were falling into place. Things started to get weird after that.

One day I called his phone and a girl picked up. It was one of the girls who was in my friend group. I was shocked, confused, and in disbelief. The phone call ended abruptly, and I wondered what was going on. I eventually had a conversation with my boyfriend at the time and he promised that nothing was going on and that he and that girl were just friends.

Over the next couple of weeks, he slowly, but surely, began to stop returning my phone calls and text messages with no explanation. My boyfriend, who I was in a committed relationship with, completely ghosted me. I don't even remember if I'd see him in school, but I know he stopped talking to me completely.

All I remember is that we ended up breaking up and one week later I found out that he was dating the girl who had picked up the phone. I was shocked but also not shocked by the behavior of the girl. This was the same girl who came up to me in the hall freshman year accusing me of saying I knew I'd win homecoming court. I wasn't very close to this girl, so while I was annoyed, that wasn't what hit me the hardest.

The thing that hurt the worst was that a couple of my best friends in my friend group knew about what was going on and never told me. These were some of the same friends who sat in the same row as me waiting for our name to be announced as homecoming court winner. They watched the betrayal unfold, listened to me complaining about my boyfriend ignoring me, but remained completely silent about the truth, and even gave me watered down advice on the topic.

I was completely left in the dark about the situation. It was confusing and hurtful. That was the beginning of the end of my friendships with several girls in my class. We fell out and when we were no longer friends, I began to find out that many of the secrets I'd told them were no longer secrets. My personal business was spread through the school as rumors, and I was even talked about and called a hoe.

As a high school kid dealing with that type of trauma, you don't really realize the depth of what you're encountering. I recognized it as drama, but it was a traumatic experience. I'd grown to trust several people and now had to question whether anybody had my best interest at heart.

I always wondered what it was that I did wrong to deserve such poor treatment from "friends". I always wondered if it was the fact that I was the one who was chosen as homecoming court winner. Did that create tension in our friend group that I was oblivious to because I won, and they didn't? If I hadn't had been chosen, would this story have unfolded any differently? That's something I'll never know.

I've wondered so many things over the years, but that situation really caused me to build walls around my heart that didn't allow me to really develop healthy relationships with women for the longest. It made me feel nervous about others being secretly in competition with me. It made me dull my shine to make others feel comfortable. It made me fear sharing my true, vulnerable self with any woman for a long time.

High school really caused me to lose trust in men and romance. It also caused me to lose trust in women as friends. I started to believe that most women were catty, messy, jealous, and could not be trusted. When it started to be uncomfortable for me to develop relationships with women who wanted to be friends with me after high school, I had to examine what had caused me to have so much anxiety around it. That reflection alone has helped me gain so much insight over time.

I realized that my experience with girls in high school caused me not to trust everybody's intentions. It caused me to go from this seemingly outgoing girl to an extremely introverted girl who didn't like dealing with large groups of people. The fear of trusting others in friendships and romance also carried over into other areas of my life.

The fear of trusting others is a tough fear to deal with. While at times it's reasonable not to trust others, it's completely unreasonable to say that nobody should be trusted.

Here are a few mindsets and beliefs that may indicate you have fear of trusting others:

- You are afraid of trusting a romantic partner
- You are paranoid and assume a partner is cheating or lying with no reasonable evidence of either
- You believe that nobody can be trusted
- You don't have anyone as an outlet for your secrets (other than a therapist or counselor) because you're afraid to trust anyone with your secrets
- You question everybody's motives and often think others are out to get you

Learning to trust other people within reason is going to help you flourish in your Promised Land. Trusting the right people is what matters. Of course, there's no real way to know if others are trustworthy or not from the start, but you have to be willing to open yourself up eventually to build healthy relationships in your Promised Land. That's why it's so important to be connected to God and pray for discernment to help you along the way.

# 3.2 *Reflecting on Your Past Trauma*

Becoming bold and courageous really takes intentional work and effort. Once you identify areas of fear in your life, it's also just as important to identify areas of trauma.

For years I struggled with anxiety and had no idea. I would go along in life and be perfectly fine until an unexpected moment of anxiety would overtake me. Anxiety would show up when I was taking an important test that really impacted my grades in school. It would also show up when I went to perform a dance routine that I had memorized perfectly but I would freeze up when it was time to shine. It would also show up when I was acting in a play and had all eyes on me, and I just froze and my mind went blank.

I'm going to walk you through a few scenarios in my life that highlighted my past traumas. My aim is to help you dig deep to discover your hidden traumas and find ways to shift your thinking and your behaviors to be more courageous when faced with fear.

During the summer before my senior year of high school, I spent time at cheerleading camp with my team. Schools from near and far would travel just to attend this camp; there were hundreds of students. We'd work on everything from cheer stunts, tumbling, and even dance routines. Dancing was always my favorite and I happened to be good at it.

During the week of camp, we all learned the same choreography routine. The camp organizers would scout out the top performers from the group and have them take center stage on the final day of camp to compete to receive an award. We learned the choreography while in massive groups, so it was easy to get lost in the crowd. The camp organizers scouted me out within the crowd and chose me as one of the finalists to perform on the final day. My teammates helped me practice and perfect the routine and I got the routine down perfectly. Then the day of the big performance came.

Dressed in my red and white mini skirt and top, with my white shoes tightly tied, and a frilly bow on top of my head, I was ready. The music started and I danced like nobody was watching until my brain realized that hundreds of people had their eyes on me, and my team was expecting me to take home the award. I cracked under pressure, missed at least an eight-count of the routine, and embarrassingly tried to recover. At that point, I'd already lost my chance at winning.

Before the routine began, my teammates were completely convinced that I was the best dancer on the floor. They were convinced that I would, without-a-doubt, take the award home. But no amount of talent could match up and win in the face of my fears and anxieties at the time. Seventeen-year-old Candace Junée felt the fear and let it cripple her. It's the same fear that kept showing up throughout my life until I identified it and intentionally faced it to dismantle it.

The fear of having all eyes on me nearly hijacked my purpose. One of the callings that I have on my life is the gift of public speaking including preaching, teaching, and giving keynote speeches. That fear still shows up every time I prepare to take the stage or pulpit whether in-person or virtual but imagine if I allowed that fear to stop me from delivering my messages.

Even after high school, I was the high achiever who everyone praised, yet I struggled when in the spotlight. As I've taken time to reflect on why I was so negatively impacted by being in the spotlight, a few of my past traumas come to mind:

- When I was crowned homecoming court winner in high school and had to walk across the floor while being booed

- Growing up in a home with family that was overly critical of my mistakes and where I was reprimanded harshly

- Being teased for the way that I looked in elementary school and junior high school

The spotlight was something I grew to hate because of my experience in it. I appeared confident, but nobody knew I was afraid. Though many of the traumas that impacted me were about my physical appearance, it really impacted my self-image and inner view of myself and my abilities. I became extremely self-critical of myself, my work, my talents, and the way that I looked.

My traumas were like an ax hacking away at the confidence I had to be able to stand tall. These traumas would even show up during my MBA program as a twenty-one-year-old woman.

The summer before my MBA program, a select few of the students in my program went to a conference that could potentially help us land internships for the next summer. The average age for everyone in the program was around thirty-two, and I was twenty-one at the time. We had to prepare an elevator pitch to share with recruiters and get it down to a tee so that we could make a great impression. We dressed up in our best suits, and in a small group of ten-to-fifteen people, practiced our elevator speech.

When it was my turn, I stood up in the middle of the circle to share my pitch, it began to flow effortlessly off my lips. That is until I got overwhelmed with the thought of everyone looking at me and I crumbled. I paused, vocalized that I forgot the rest of it and I was so nervous. It was too much for me. I had to sit down after I not-so-confidently finished my elevator pitch. I was embarrassed, but even after that hiccup everyone in the group was telling me how great it was, and they couldn't tell that I was nervous.

I presented well, but my view of myself made me crumble because I was not truly confident within. When it came time to go into the career fair with hundreds of companies lined up with their booths, I grew even more anxious. Instead of seeing myself as a powerful, young, twenty-one-year-old hanging with the big dogs, I felt like my age was a disqualifier of my talent.

Deep down I feared that I would not be good enough and that, ultimately, I would be rejected. This was something that continuously came up in my life. I lacked confidence, boldness, and courage simply because I was not able to view myself properly. I was not able to truly view myself the way that God viewed me. Over time I've learned that regardless of my decisions, God views me with love, compassion, and forgiveness. He reminded me that I am not defined by the decisions of my past nor what people think of me. The more I began to accept God's true love for me, I was able to evolve into more of a courageously confident woman.

Reflecting on the areas where fear has become a part of your life and being honest with yourself about the impact of past traumas is a bold and courageous decision to make. It takes courage to look at some of your most painful moments and decide that they will no longer control you. The work you're doing now to be intentional about your reflections is work that you are going to thank yourself for later. The people in your Promised Land will be so much better off because of it.

Many of you, like me, have experienced traumas you can easily recognize and point back to. You may also have other traumas that have been hiding and covered up for years. You might have even blocked them out of your mind like I did. It wasn't until I was in my mid-twenties when I revisited the domestic violence I experienced at home as a kid. Someone asked me if my father ever put his hands on my mom and it was almost like a light bulb popped on and I remembered the painful trauma of my past.

I personally believe that, had I not uncovered those wounds, I would not have been able to experience the clarity and freedom I'm able to experience now. Addressing your trauma and being intentional about healing from it is one of the boldest steps of courage you can take.

Our traumas shape us, our world view, our self-view, our identity, and ultimately our confidence. Though we are not the ones who initially caused us harm and pain, we are the ones left to pick up the pieces. It's our job to take responsibility for what happened to us while also recognizing that it was not our fault.

I challenge you to face your trauma by reflecting on the areas that you may have experienced deep hurt, pain, betrayal, or any other traumatic experience. As mentioned before, the goal for this part is to have you uncover, reflect, and acknowledge before taking action to heal.

Answering the following questions may help you uncover areas where you have experienced trauma.

When approaching the following questions, you should not only answer the question but ask yourself, "How has this impacted me?"

## Here are the questions for your reflection:

1. What traumatic experiences have you dealt with during your childhood?

2. Have you ever experienced physical or verbal abuse?

3. Were you neglected by a parent, loved one, or spouse?

4. Was one or more of your parents absent from your life or inconsistent with their presence in your life?

5. Have you witnessed a parent or loved one struggle with alcoholism or drug addictions?

6. Were you abandoned or neglected as a child?

7. Were you ever molested or touched inappropriately as a child?

8. Have you ever experienced sexual assault or rape?

9. Have you ever experienced betrayal or rumors?

10. Did you ever experience the divorce or separation of your parents or caregivers?

11. What times in your life have you experienced fear and anxiety?

Answering these questions is a bold decision. Remember not to rush through this exercise. You owe it to yourself to take this exercise seriously. Don't run from it, my friend. Remember that reflecting on your trauma and facing it will help you thrive on your way to and in the Promised Land.

# 4 *Bold & Courageous Healing*

To walk in your God-given calling and authority, you need internal healing. Doing the work of reflecting on your past traumas may have seemed overwhelming, overbearing, and downright painful, but I am proud of you for doing the work. The truth is if you don't deal with it now, it's going to find a way to expose itself in your Promised Land or even worse, attempt to hinder you from getting there.

The next step on the journey to becoming more bold and courageous is to heal from the pain of your past. This chapter is dedicated to helping you start (or continue) your healing journey and develop a plan to heal from the internal wounds.

At this point in your life, your experiences have shaped who you are and how you show up. Your job now is to take responsibility for it and shift what needs to be shifted so that you can become the highest version of yourself.

The highest version of yourself exists in a place of peace where your trauma no longer has the power over you that it once had. Our goal of exposing past pain is never to remain in a place where you beat yourself up or sulk in the negativity of your past. Rather, it's so that you can take your power back and walk in your true power.

The summer after I graduated from college, I entered a journey of intense healing from my past. Just a few months prior, I had experienced one of the most traumatic things that had ever happened to me.

At the time I was finishing the final year of my MBA program and felt completely alone. I'd just broken up with my longtime boyfriend who I'd spend most of my time with, and I didn't really have a supportive community of people around me at the time. I decided to go on a trip with a guy who wanted to date me, Darnell. I flew all the way to Baltimore, Maryland in the middle of winter and experienced a weekend of bliss with a guy who was a major romantic interest. Not only was I able to spend my birthday weekend with Darnell, but I was also excited that I didn't have to spend Valentine's Day weekend alone.

In the wee hours of the morning of my twenty-third birthday, I was sexually assaulted and raped by Darnell's friend while intoxicated. To this day, I still don't know if I was drugged or not. I can only remember bits and pieces of what happened to me. Darnell's friend, though he had been with another girl all weekend, took advantage of me while in his home that we were crashing at. I woke up the next morning with flashbacks of what happened and tried to convince myself that it was all a bad dream. As soon as I saw the man who raped me in the morning, I could see from the smirk on his face and his extreme attention to detail regarding my existence, that it was not a dream. He stared at me awkwardly until Darnell and I gathered our belongings and left.

I was too afraid to tell Darnell what his friend had done to me. I really liked Darnell, but I also hadn't spent a ton of time with him to know him intimately or his mannerisms. Because of the domestic violence I'd witnessed as a kid, my biggest fear was doing something that would trigger a man to hit me. So, I kept silent about his friend for fear of what he could potentially do to harm me physically while in his care. Not only that, but I was also ashamed of what happened to me. I felt like I was dirty, as if this was something I had asked for. I honestly didn't even recognize it as rape until much later down the line. I just knew that what he had done was wrong.

I'd never thought that I'd be the girl who was raped, let alone sharing the story of sexual assault. But it's something I know that many people have experienced, and I've learned that my story has power and purpose to help others heal.

My healing journey started when I got back to St. Louis after that trip. Alone in my apartment and feeling as empty as I've ever felt in life, I dropped to my knees and surrendered my life to God, again. I didn't have an outlet or a safe space where I could share for fear of being called a hoe. But in that moment, I allowed myself to lay all my pain out in a verbal conversation with God. I honestly didn't understand why God had let this happen to me if He loved me so much.

Despite my frustration and confusion, I told God something that I'll never forget. "I don't know the purpose you have planned for my life, but I know that this is not it. I'm tired of going about my life my way, so I'm giving up my plan for yours. Nothing is off limits. Whatever you want me to do, my life is yours," I said.

My relationship with parents caused me to expect reprimands and harsh criticism from God. Instead, God's response to me was always with love and compassion. He always made it clear that He had the ability to heal what I could not heal on my own.

What happened to me caused me to view myself as damaged and unwanted. It made me wonder what it was about me that made this man take advantage of me as if I had no value. It made me wonder what I did to make him think it was okay to touch me and force himself on me. It made me wonder if it was what I wore, how I carried myself, or how friendly and polite I had been to him in conversation the day before upon first meeting him.

The trauma had me looking at myself like I was the problem, when, in reality, I was not the problem. Sometimes we take the blame for the trauma that happens to us, but it's not our job to do that. It's our job to assess what happened and heal from it.

Your healing journey is for you, but your healing may also help others heal, too. The first time I openly shared that I'd experienced rape, I did it on social media. I shared my story on a platform called Periscope. At the time Periscope enabled live video streaming right from your device to an audience of people across the globe. At the time this was a brand-new popularized feature that had never been widely done before by a tech company. The live streaming concept eventually got adopted and even more popularized by major social media platforms like Instagram®, Facebook ®, and TikTok®.

Once I shared my story live on Periscope, there was no going back. So many people thanked me for my vulnerability and some privately shared with me how much it had impacted them. Over the next year or so, I opened up even more about my experience with rape on social media in my Facebook and Instagram posts. Both Facebook and Instagram were more widely used than Periscope at the time, so when I shared on these platforms, my story had a much wider reach and audience.

This time, my inbox was filled with so many private messages from women of all ages who had gone through similar experiences. This was prior to the #MeToo movement, and so many women were telling me how they thought I was so courageous to share. That was when I seriously realized the impact of speaking my truth and not hiding from it. When I shared my experiences, I shared it with a purpose after I had gone through the initial stages of healing.

When I started my healing journey, it was focused on the most recent trauma I had experienced, rape. While I started to unpack how that experience made me feel, it began to open wounds that I'd been suffering from for years. The rape negatively impacted my self-confidence. It took me to an all-time low, but I had to dig into it to heal.

When spending more time reflecting, I started to see that I had been struggling with confidence issues and low self-esteem for years. It started long before I was assaulted. I started to see that because of my low self-confidence, negative body image, and lack of affirmation from my parents, I'd been searching for love and acceptance in all the wrong places. I had grown to hate myself and the way that I looked and was seeking affirmation and acceptance from romantic relationships with guys.

During my senior year of high school, I started dating one of my closest guy friends, Malik. At first, I was adamant about us staying friends, but he consistently pursued me, and I finally gave in to saying yes to dating him. I felt like it was safe and almost as if I knew he would be different from other guys and that I wouldn't get hurt. We dated for a couple of months, and he slowly started to ignore my calls and texts. Malik broke up with me right around my birthday and that next week I found out he had asked one of my ex-best friends to prom. Of course, my heart was shattered, and my feelings were hurt because I was let down by someone I trusted.

I remember feeling terrible after that happened. I couldn't sleep. I couldn't eat. Not only was I without a prom date, but most other guys in the school had already had a plan for who they were asking to prom. I was left without a date, and I was completely embarrassed. I felt so low, picked over, and like I was not good enough in any guy's eyes. I did my best to bounce back and ended up going to prom with a guy from another school who I'd been getting to know over the past couple of years.

I literally hopped from that one relationship to another, never truly allowing myself the time to heal. Relationships were where I felt most valuable. My prom date, Jeremiah, became my newest relationship. We dated during the final semester of my senior year and even through our first semester of college. We had met each other's parents, were sexually intimate, shared that we both loved one another, but he kept insisting that he did not like titles. He refused to commit to the title of boyfriend and girlfriend, but he made it clear to me that we were in a committed relationship.

Our relationship continued, and it pretty much felt like we were boyfriend and girlfriend. Of course, Jeremiah wasn't okay with me dating other people, so I grew tired of that quickly since we didn't have that public title. I'd ask him questions like, "If I'm only dating you and you're only dating me, then why is it a problem for us to use the title of boyfriend and girlfriend?" That conversation never really got us anywhere, but he would always soothe my concerns and remind me that he loved me, and the title didn't mean anything to him. We both went away to separate colleges, but we continued to stay in our relationship. I'd even travel to his school to visit him whenever he wanted to see me.

Then one day during my freshman year of college, while I was sitting in my Physics class, I received a phone call from Jeremiah. I sent the call to voicemail and noticed that he had left a voicemail message for me. I figured it must have been something very important or something that had gone wrong because this was not typical of him. I rushed to my dorm room to listen to the voicemail while sitting in silence.

I put my phone on speaker and played the recording. I soon found out that he had not intentionally called me. It was an accidental phone call and I overheard what was going on in the room he was in. I heard him and another woman being sexually intimate.

That day my heart was crushed. I had been praying to God and asking for signs on what to do about this guy for months, and that voicemail was all I needed. It was almost as if God allowed that to happen so I could know the truth. I felt like a fool. All this time I thought I should have been paying attention to the signs and what he told me. The reality is, if a man wanted to be with me and truly loved me, he would not have to hide our relationship. If he loved me and wanted to be with me, he would commit to me. For some reason while in that relationship, I could not see things clearly. It was almost as if I was blinded by "love" and being accepted by him, regardless of how he treated me and made me feel.

After that relationship, I began to pick up the pieces and recognize that I was valuable. I started to see that I deserved to be treated better by men. For a while, I completely took a break from dating guys, but I still found myself in and out of relationships until I was in my early twenties. I'd been in and out of relationships up until my experience with being raped in college.

It's hard to look back at the pain of your past. It's also very easy to judge yourself for your past decisions. It's easy to criticize your past behaviors, but I'm here to remind you to give yourself grace.

It takes courage to recognize what went wrong and how you could have responded better. Your past decisions should not define how you treat yourself in the present. Regardless of your decisions and what happened to you, you are still an extremely valuable person and an asset to society.

Of course, I wanted to tell myself how dumb and naive it was for me to believe lies. Of course, I wanted to tell myself how it was my fault for allowing a man to treat me that way. But I could not do it. I had to recognize that I was growing, learning, and becoming more of who I am. There was no reason for me to punish myself for my decisions and what I could not control. Over the years, I've had to courageously make the decision not to be mean to myself. I'll talk more on treating yourself with kindness later in this book.

This was not the last time I experienced betrayal and cheating in a relationship, though. After college, I began working in corporate America and really started focusing on my career. During that time, I started dating a guy I'd known since childhood, Jalen. Though I had honestly given up on romance, I thought this guy would be different. Jalen was a seemingly wholesome, Christian man who regularly attended church.

We had a lot of things in common and we connected a lot about our faith in God. We really enjoyed spending time together and it got to the point where we were dating and had a moment of sexual intimacy — still with no title for our relationship.

When I asked Jalen about his intentions with our relationship, he began to tell me something that felt very familiar to me. He told me he was not interested in being in a committed relationship at the time. Since it felt like I was being courted, I was confused.

In previous relationships, like with Jeremiah, I'd been afraid to ask about the status of our relationship. I'd feel guilty for asking because it was almost as if I was convinced that I didn't have the right to ask about a relationship status if the man didn't bring it up first. I'd be afraid to tell a guy that I desired commitment and did not want to settle for a situationship. I got over that fear and decided to speak up. So, I got the courage to tell him that I did not want to be sexually intimate with someone who I was not in a committed relationship with. I told him that I was okay if our relationship needed to change, but I did not want to continue a relationship with someone who did not want to commit to me.

I walked away from the relationship-defining conversation with Jalen feeling empowered. I was okay with being single and waiting for someone who would be willing to commit to me because I deserved that. Ironically, just days after that phone conversation, Jalen called me and asked me to be his girlfriend. I paused and asked him if he was sure because I didn't want him to commit just because I wanted him to, rather I wanted him to know for himself that this was what he wanted. He insisted that this was what he wanted and that was the beginning of our relationship.

Jalen and I continued a long-distance relationship for months and even spent time with each other's families. He quickly shared with me that he loved me and that he wanted to marry me within the near future. I was willing to make it work because I finally found a guy who was communicating his long-term commitment to me. We would see each other once or twice a month, and slowly, but surely, I began to see a different side of Jalen, both on the phone and in person.

Though Jalen would post about me openly on social media and share with the world how I was his beautiful queen who he adored, he treated me very differently privately. Jalen began to be very verbally and emotionally abusive. It was extremely traumatic for me. He would say things often to belittle me. He would raise his voice and be extremely negative.

As time went on in our relationship, our Instagram-perfect relationship began to crumble. One day while I was visiting Jalen, I had his phone and a message popped up from another woman. He had her name saved as a nickname with heart emojis. I began to read the text message thread. Jalen had been having inappropriate conversations with this woman for months during our relationship. I found nearly ten different women that he had been inappropriately talking to and cheating on me with.

I was livid. I gathered my belongings to head to the airport. I tried my best to hide my anger because I did not want to make a scene. As we headed to his car, I couldn't bring myself to say a word to him and he kept begging me to tell him what was wrong. I never told him exactly what I saw, but I confronted him about cheating on me. He sat there in the car completely stunned and shocked, looking like a deer in headlights. At this point I couldn't hold my anger any longer… I went completely off. This was not how I deserved to be treated. I told him that we were no longer in a relationship and that he needed to take me to the airport.

As Jalen started driving to the airport in silence, he began trying to apologize and saying things like, "I loved you so much, it scared me," and, "It was too good to be true, so I wanted to make sure I knew it was real and that I couldn't find anybody else better, but now I know I have you and I don't need anything better."

I didn't care anymore. All I cared about was getting to the airport and leaving this relationship for good. But with Jalen's controlling, manipulative ways, somehow that didn't happen. As he was driving, I told him I didn't want to be with him, and he started to refuse to take me to the airport. He insisted on me giving him another chance and suggested that I pray while we were still together so that God would heal our relationship. Completely frustrated, burnt out, and confused, I sat in the car praying that God would heal the relationship with this man who was treating me terribly.

Deep down I knew I didn't want to be with Jalen, but I remained in the relationship because I felt stuck, and I thought there was a chance that he would get better. Our relationship continued and I even celebrated my birthday with him in a new city. For my birthday, he took me on a romantic dinner date to a restaurant in a fancy part of the town. Jalen got up to go to the restroom and came back with a surprise cake with candles glaring. As he walked across the restaurant floor beautifully singing John Legend's song, "All of Me," all I could think was, "I hope he's not about to propose." I was so scared and shocked at the same time.

Everyone in the restaurant was staring at Jalen walking over to me. It looked like a classic proposal setup that would have been such an 'Instagrammable' moment. I was completely caught by surprise. By the time Jalen got to me with the cake, I had already devised a plan so as not to embarrass him. I had decided that if he popped the question, I'd tell him "Yes" at the restaurant and after I'd leave and tell him I couldn't marry him.

John Legend's "All of Me" would forever be ruined in my eyes, but thank God, that birthday surprise did not end with a proposal. *Whew.*

I believe that experience served its purpose. It was a huge wakeup call to me that I did not want to be in that relationship and that I needed to find a way out. I stayed with Jalen for a few months until I started to see that I really deserved better. I spent a lot of time praying and fasting, asking God to help me make whatever decision I should make.

For the longest time, I could not find the courage to tell Jalen that I did not want to be with him. I felt like I needed a really convincing explanation as to why I didn't want to be with him and like I needed to have a debate prepared just to express how I felt. But then one day, I just woke up. I realized I did not owe him an explanation. All I knew was that this relationship no longer served me, and it was not healthy for me to be in. I knew I could not become the best version of myself while being in this relationship. I was able to step away from the feelings of guilt for believing I deserved better. Instead, I made my decision without consulting with him about what we were going to do.

As I walked out of the gym that morning, I picked up the phone to call Jalen. "I don't want to be with you anymore," were the last words I said to him. The relationship ended there, and it was the beginning of a brand-new journey of self-discovery and self-love.

After my experience with being raped in college and with yet another traumatic relationship in the books, I had to really reflect on all the things that made me feel like I was not good enough. I had to figure out why I didn't value myself highly enough in relationships with men that caused me to settle with abuse and mistreatment.

I started to see that for so long I placed my self-worth in being in a relationship with a guy. Though I never entered any of the relationships by consciously thinking, "I don't love myself. I'll feel way better about myself if a guy loves me," that's what I was doing. I was willing to deal with nonsense like cheating from men just to be accepted, loved, or viewed by others as accepted and loved.

Healing from your past trauma is so crucial when it comes to your purpose and your Promised Land. Sometimes we take on so much and experience so much in life and it doesn't have a space to go, so it remains trapped inside of us. Trauma, hurt, and pain, if not dealt with, can turn into bitterness, anger, stress, anxiety, and a slew of other emotions and feelings.

If you're not careful, you can take out your frustrations on others or even yourself when, in reality, that's not how you like to behave. There may be ways that you currently behave that you don't even realize are linked to unhealed trauma and wounds; but your healing journey will be worth the pain of facing the past hurt because you'll be better on the other side.

The first step on the journey to healing is forgiveness. Once you've recognized what happened to you, it's important to release yourself from the pain it has caused you.

Forgiving someone does not mean that what they did to you was right. Forgiveness means you are making a personal decision to release yourself from the bondage and control it once had over you. It's not excusing what they did to you. Forgiveness acknowledges the pain and the truth of what happened. Forgiveness allows you to say, "I'm no longer holding that person to the pain of what they did to me. I'm choosing to no longer be angry and bitter because of what happened."

This type of forgiveness takes practice. It honestly doesn't make much sense when you first look at it. Why would you let someone get away with what they did to hurt you whether intentionally or unintentionally? Let's be honest, with situations so horrific like rape, murder, abuse, molestation, betrayal, or slander, it seems like the person guilty of the offense deserves violence, bitterness, and anger in return. It doesn't make logical sense to say, "I'll let you get away with this," but forgiveness is necessary for your healing. You're not really letting that person get away, rather, you're taking back the control and choosing to release them into the freedom that forgiveness has to offer.

Oftentimes, when someone has done something wrong against you, they may not even feel the guilt of what they've done. There's a chance that many of them would walk away and live their lives as if they never did anything to hurt you. They may even forget about what happened because it may not have been that significant to them. That's exactly why forgiveness is not about the person who hurt you.

Forgiving others is about you healing from what happened to you and choosing to be better after. You are the one dealing with and holding onto the memories and feelings of what happened to you. You are the one who is most deeply impacted by the pain of the situation. That's why it's your responsibility to forgive so that you can heal.

The thing that made it easier for me to forgive has been my relationship with God. Follow me through this. I had always been a Christian since I was seven years old. I consciously gave my life to Jesus and felt the spirit of God that was very real in my life. As I grew up and went through high school and college, I made many wrong decisions and willingly took part in sin. Whether it was having sex before marriage, telling a white lie, gossiping, or any other negative decision I'd made, I hadn't always been perfect. I blatantly disobeyed God and did not always make decisions that aligned with God's version of righteousness.

When I began my healing journey after rape and I surrendered my life to God in my college apartment, I started to accept God's love and forgiveness. Every time I felt like I'd made such terrible decisions, God did not reprimand me or make me feel like I was a horrible person. He made it clear that He loved me and that I was forgiven. When I came to God, I would repent and tell Him what I'd done wrong, and He would graciously grant me forgiveness. I was never made to feel like I was not worthy of His love nor like I was a terrible human being.

I had to learn how to extend that same forgiveness to others. If God could forgive me though He saw all of the wrong and many offenses I'd done against Him and others, surely, I could forgive others.

So where did I start with my journey of forgiveness? With the help of counselors and mentors, I started with their advice to be intentional about addressing my pain. I started with a list of people who hurt me. I started with my siblings, my parents, the girls who I was friends with during high school, the past painful relationships I'd been in, the men who sexually assaulted me, and many others who caused me pain. It took time to process, but I wrote out a list of what I was forgiving them for, specifically.

For some of the more painful traumas I experienced, like rape, I wrote a letter directly to that person to release the anger and frustration I had within me. I was able to write things like, "Though I know you planned to rape me, I forgive you for taking advantage of me." Writing that letter was rough, but at least the pain of what happened to me was no longer inside of me, ripping away at my heart and soul.

For some of the people in your life, it may be helpful to have a conversation with them about the experience and what happened. We will talk more about how to have bold and courageous conversations to bring healing in chapter nine. But for others, you may not be able to have a conversation with them because you don't have their contact information, they may be deceased, or it may not be necessary or fruitful. It's up to you to decide whether a conversation is needed, but I recommend having conversations if you know that you need to continue a relationship with them in the future. However, everything does not need to be said and you don't need to go into the situation expecting an apology.

You may be thinking that it might be hard to forgive someone who is not sorry or is not apologizing. However, whether you have a conversation with the person or not, you will still need to forgive them. Chances are, you probably won't get an apology from everybody who hurt you. Forgiveness is not about getting an apology, it's about your healing and your ultimate freedom.

Sometimes when we experience intense trauma and pain, we have a desire for revenge. Let me be clear that it's natural for you to want to seek justice after something so terrible happened, however justice and revenge are two different things. Revenge is based on the desire to repay evil for evil. If you desire to get revenge, it can be an indicator that you are still dealing with unforgiveness.

This all may seem like it's crazy, but, if you're comfortable with concepts like karma, why be uncomfortable with the concept of forgiveness? As a Christian woman, I have grown to learn that God is the one who fights for me. Here's what I believe:

> "Do not say, 'I'll pay you back for this wrong!' Wait for the LORD, and he will avenge you" (Proverbs 20:22 NIV).

> "The LORD will fight for you; you need only to be still" (Exodus 14:14 NIV).

Don't blame yourself for what happened to you. What happened to you was wrong. It was not your fault. Yes, you should have been safe and protected, but you were not. That's not your fault and you are not to blame for letting what happened to you happen to you. We are spiritual beings with physical bodies, but we also have a mind, a soul, and emotions. When we are in unsafe situations there are many things at play that impact our responses. Sometimes we are in a situation where we don't realize people are not safe for us, and at other times we are aware that we are in unsafe situations, but we endure the situations out of fear or some other reason. However, you should never make yourself feel bad for not making a decision other than the one you made. It is not your job to be at blame or feel shameful or guilty about what *happened to you*.

Now that we've talked about forgiving others, it's time to jump into the topic of forgiving yourself before we get back to forgiving others. Shame, guilt, and condemnation will keep you from living in the Promised Land and existing as the highest version of yourself.

Shame, guilt, and condemnation all come from feelings within. They are all byproducts of you not forgiving yourself or others. Sure, you've made some questionable decisions over the years. We all have. Sure, you have inflicted pain on yourself because of some of your decisions, but you should not be holding yourself hostage because of those decisions. Many of the decisions you made were because you were not emotionally or mentally developed enough to behave differently. Some of them were simply because what was happening happened so fast, you were under a ton of stress, or there was no real way for you to escape the situation. There are so many factors that impacted your past decisions.

You need to give yourself some grace. Give yourself grace so that you can stop blaming yourself for what happened to you. You do not have to feel ashamed of what happened to you, either. You are not alone. You and I experienced trauma, just like countless others.

Shame will make you feel like you're living under the shadow of your trauma. It will make you feel like you can never overcome your past decisions and pain. Shame is something that you can control. Nobody can make you feel shameful about something you have decided to take power over.

For example, let's say your biological parents were drug addicts and you had to be raised by adopted parents. Maybe you were teased growing up with kids saying things like, "That's why your mama left you for drugs!" or "Those aren't even your real parents." Maybe even in adulthood you had an abusive partner who said things like, "See that's what happens when you aren't raised by your real parents." Imagine hearing hurtful things your entire life and feeling ashamed of your truth. Imagine being made to feel like what happened to you is an indication of who you are or your brilliance.

When it comes to shame, you can take your power back. You have the ability to shift your perspective and recognize that you are an amazing human being and that what happened to you or what others say about you does not define you.

Shame can make you hide your true version of yourself. Usually, I see shame impact people specifically with their personality. What's really happening is that shame is causing you to think differently about yourself, so in turn, you show up differently.

Let's say you're a talkative person and you've been told your entire life that you talk too much. Instead of being the extroverted, talkative person you once were, you don't want to talk so much, so you show up in rooms and spaces as a quiet, timid person though you have lots to say. Over time you've conditioned yourself to not speak up for fear of being judged and because you're ashamed that you are a talkative person. Your personality now becomes impacted by your thoughts of being ashamed.

Shame can also shift your thoughts and impact your behaviors. Let's take another example. Maybe you were called a "whore" by others because of your openness to explore sexuality. You hated the way that made you feel and now you feel ashamed of your past decisions. Now you don't want to be judged or make other people think you're a whore, so you watch what you wear and even what you say. Deep down, you're living under the shadow of shame, and you shift your decisions because of it.

Shame really impacts your mental health and well-being. Especially for victims of sexual assault, molestation, and abuse, shame will even make you feel dirty or less than, as if you are not good enough. It may impact the way you think about yourself and the decisions that you make with things that have nothing to do with sexuality or abuse.

When you forgive yourself for your past decisions and understand that you are not held down to what you did or what happened to you, you can experience another level of freedom. Shame does not have to hold you back, and you do not have to feel guilty.

Guilt is a bestie to shame. There may have been times when you blatantly did things that you wish you could have done differently. That's usually where you'll find guilt. Guilt comes from regretting your decisions or for accepting the blame for something that occurred. You're made to feel like you're responsible for a negative outcome of a situation.

Guilt is something that will hold you back from becoming your best self. Guilt literally is a weight holding you down, trying its best to keep you away from your purpose. But dealing with and overcoming guilt will help you to walk more freely into who you are called to be. Living under the weight of guilt will have you rehearsing memories of the past, wishing you could have done something differently, and feeling like you're not good enough or deserving of good things because of it.

When you feel guilty, whether you did something horrible in the past, or you were made to feel guilty because of blame, it will make you feel like you don't deserve good things. It'll make you feel like karma is going to come back and bite you, so you live in a continuous state of fear and expectancy to be disappointed by the world. Breaking free from guilt will help you walk even more deeply in your calling. It's important to understand that you have the right to change and evolve into a different person that makes different decisions in the future. Give yourself permission to evolve and move forward without the weight of your past and decisions of yesterday.

When dealing with the rape I experienced, it was so hard to pick up the pieces of my life. I felt extremely broken, shattered, and lost. I felt like my life was moving in slow motion. I was preparing to graduate from undergrad and get my MBA at the same time…surely, I should have been excited, right? I was far from excited because I was just going through the motions so that I wouldn't completely lose my mind.

I remained silent about what happened to me for so long because I felt ashamed of what happened to me. I felt guilty for the decisions I made that led up to what happened to me. I mulled over and analyzed my decisions time and time again. So many thoughts were swirling through my head: *What could I have done differently? This would have never happened if I had never taken that trip. I shouldn't have trusted the guy I was dating so easily. I should have never been so nice to him. I should have not worn such a tight-fitting dress.*

The thoughts were endless. But there came a point when I had to free myself from shame and guilt to get the healing I desperately needed and wanted. A part of that healing journey started with forgiving someone who I felt did not deserve my forgiveness — my rapist.

Forgiveness is a pretty crazy concept. How do you forgive someone who raped you? How do you allow yourself to say in your mind that you're releasing that person from what they did to cause so much harm to you? Remember earlier I said: forgiveness is not saying that what someone else did to you was not right. It's just releasing yourself from the bondage of it having the control it had over you.

I no longer wanted the weight of what happened to me to control my decisions or what I thought about myself. Forgiving the man who raped me in college helped me to free myself from the guilt and the shame that was attached to what happened. I'm not going to lie, it was very hard to do, but I had to realize that forgiveness is a journey. It's something I had to do not just once, but I had to extend him the grace of forgiveness every time the thought of holding onto the pain came to my mind.

As a Christian, the next principle I'm about to share is one that really helped me extend forgiveness. I truly value having a healthy relationship with God, and the Bible is clear that when I forgive others, God will forgive me. Here are a couple of verses that help me understand God's perspective on forgiveness:

> "And whenever you stand praying, forgive, if you have anything against anyone, so that your Father also who is in heaven may forgive you your trespasses" (Mark 11:25 ESV).

"Then Peter came to Jesus and asked, 'Lord, how many times shall I forgive my brother or sister who sins against me? Up to seven times?' Jesus answered, 'I tell you, not seven times, but seventy-seven times' (Matthew 18:21-22 NIV).

The Bible is clear that we should forgive. It's clear that it should be a continuous process simply by the number of times Jesus says to forgive. Seventy times seven is 490 times. I believe this expresses the true work and intentionality it takes to forgive someone. It's not enough to say I forgive someone once, it's imperative for it to be a continuous journey.

In mid-2021, after recovering from another failed romantic relationship, I was hit with a load of new trauma. I promised myself not to be closed off to dating because of past failed relationships, so I gave dating another try.

I met a guy who started to pursue me and take me out on dates. He presented himself as a calm, gentle-spirited man who was interested in "dating with a purpose, settling down, getting married, and having kids." After several dates, I felt comfortable enough being alone with him, but I didn't expect what would happen to me. The first time we were alone together he forced himself on me and raped me.

Though I'd been raped before, this time was different because it was with someone who was actively pursuing me and communicating that sex was not his interest or intent. We were mutually interested in getting to know each other. I clearly communicated my boundaries around sex and that I was not interested in having sex, but he never honored my clear and consistent "no" once we were alone together. After he raped me, he completely ghosted me and stopped communicating with me.

This time, the rape left me completely shattered and anxious. After all I had been through with dating men in the past and the abuse I survived, this happened. I felt completely empty and picked over. The same feelings I had from the previous rape emerged yet again. I was so angry that this man treated me so poorly and I didn't understand how this could happen to me. I was the girl who was obeying God and doing things "right". I was the girl who did my best to steer far away from sin, but I could not understand how this happened to me. I felt like I was uncovered, and it made me question why God would allow something so terrible to happen to me.

This happened to me at a point when I had been following God, walking in obedience to God regarding my calling, building my successful businesses, and had grown much closer to God than I was in college. My mind was overwhelmed with the thought of it, but I had to remind myself that God was there with me the entire time. I was angry that I was such a target for the enemy's plans. I was upset that I was completely blindsided and felt unprepared to deal with this when my business demanded so much out of me at the time. I couldn't even think straight or give my clients the attention they deserved. I mentally checked out for a while.

For days after the rape, I sat there shocked, confused, nervous, anxious, and upset. I couldn't eat. I struggled to sleep at night. My heart felt like it was ripped out of my chest. I had panic attacks and felt like I could pass out at any moment. I was nervous anytime I saw a man that even closely resembled his build and physique, and everyone wearing masks to protect themselves from COVID-19 didn't help my case. My mind kept running through the vivid scenes in my head, and even worse, this time I could remember every moment of it.

Looking back at the situation, I realized this man manipulated me to trust him just to get what he wanted. He went out of his way to share a version of himself with me that was far from the truth. This experience with rape was even more traumatic than the first. I felt like death was knocking at my door and wanted to take me out. I felt like this plan of the enemy was designed for me to abandon God. I felt like this situation was to attack my boldness and courage, but I decided that the enemy could not win this one.

I realized that this time *was different.* I was a different Candace Junée. I recognized that now I had been equipped with a different level of faith and confidence in God. Now I had been equipped with a new level of authority that I didn't know I had when I was the twenty-three-year-old Candace. This time, I took my power back and moved differently than I did before. This time I made the decision to speak out to my friends and family to let them know I was not okay. This time I had people covering me in prayer consistently the entire time. This time I intentionally sought out deliverance and healing ministry at church. This time, I took my power back, chose to report the sexual assault to the police, and began warfare against the enemy.

I'm not sure of the exact thing that switched to help me shift from a place of overwhelm to a place of power and authority, but I'm convinced that it was prayer and deliverance that helped the most. Of course, I'm still healing and recovering from these traumas, but I'm healing from a place of power and my God-given authority. I know the power that my words and prayers have. I know the authority that my prayers and decrees have over the plots and schemes of the enemy. I had to choose to step into that power instead of allowing the enemy to intimidate me out of it.

The hardest part of trauma other than surviving it is forgiveness. The thing I struggled with most was forgiveness. I was quicker to forgive myself, but I really struggled to begin the journey of forgiving this man who hurt me. Forgiveness takes lots of work and intentional effort. Again, forgiveness must be a continuous journey. It's hard, but it gets easier with every moment you choose to forgive those who don't deserve your forgiveness. That's the only way to move forward and become the best version of yourself.

No matter what you've been through. God will be with you. That's the same promise that God gave to Joshua, and it's a promise that you can personalize for yourself. Your journey to the Promised Land will come with many battles. Just because you're choosing to follow God, that does not mean you are exempt from experiencing hurt and pain. But never forget that you are fighting every battle from a place of victory and authority with your God-given power.

Sometimes we deal with people based on our frustrations and irritations with them from our past pain. For example, for years

I would not pick up the phone when my father was calling me. I would ignore his phone calls. Or when I talked to him, I'd be so bitter that I'd be annoyed with him, and you could hear it in the tone of my voice. I didn't like my dad that much because of the pain he caused me and my family in the past, so I allowed my pain to keep me from forgiving him. After graduating college, I had to live with my parents briefly. One day my dad and I got into an argument about something, and my dad completely went off on me. I stood up for myself and exchanged some words with him and he kicked me out of their house.

So, I left with nowhere to go but to a family member's house nearby. After staying with a family member for a few nights, my cousin gently confronted me and told me I needed to deal with the situation at home. I told her how it was extremely hard to deal with my dad. I shared with her that my dad had done some unforgivable things over the years and how I was so fed up. I'll never forget what she told me next. She told me that there are times when you are going to be annoyed and frustrated, but my job was to forgive my father daily because he didn't realize the impact of the pain that he caused me. She told me this: every time he upsets me, treat him with love and verbally say "I forgive him". I didn't have to speak these words directly to my father, but instead, I was able to verbally say "I forgive him" every time I wanted to choose unforgiveness instead.

When you're first going through the journey of forgiveness, one of the hardest things to do is forgive someone who you felt did not deserve your forgiveness. My dad was one of those people. He had done a laundry list of things that made me feel so angry. He had done so much to cause pain to me, my mom, and my family. It was continuous, but I had to begin to forgive him so that my relationship with him would eventually change.

Though I had bitterness in my heart toward my father, I had to shift from focusing on the negative to focusing on the positive. I definitely loved and appreciated my father, and I did not want to discount that. I appreciated the father he was and understood that he was a broken man who fathered the way he knew how. I appreciated that he never chose to walk away from our family, and I appreciated the hard work he did to financially support my family. When initially looking at the situation, I felt like the bad completely outweighed the good, and it did not warrant me to forgive him. However, I had to realize that my healing was connected to forgiving him, though I felt he did not deserve it. I mean, after all, how could a father treat his kids so poorly? How could a husband abuse his wife? My journey of forgiveness with my dad has been one of the toughest, but I'm grateful I learned to continuously forgive him long before he ever issued a sincere apology.

It took years for my father to take accountability for his actions, but, eventually, he did. My father apologized to me and my siblings for his actions and for the abusive environment we grew up in. He owned up to it, and I appreciated that. We can't change the past, and I cannot continue to hold my father to his past. My father has changed so much since he's made intentional efforts to be a better man. My dad stopped putting his hands on my mom when we were younger, and the aggression eased up a lot over time.

Now, as an adult, I know for sure that God has been working on him. You can tell that he makes the effort to be a better father. He even texts scriptures and encouraging words at the perfect moments. While my relationship with my dad is not perfect, it has shifted so much. I now pick up more often when he calls, and he shows up at my house whenever I need a handyman. He also listens to me more. I've seen God change his life for the better in so many ways, and I am forever grateful that our relationship has drastically improved since making the decision to forgive him continuously. It's still a continuous journey. Forgiveness was initially a struggle for me with people who I felt completely belittled me, took advantage of me, or even spread gossip about me. I personally felt they were not worthy of forgiveness. I put them in a box I called "trifflin' people" who are just ruthless, selfish, and absurd. For so long, I could not stand their guts. When their names or stories were brought up, sometimes I'd get furious and other times I'd brush it off and act as if they were insignificant. However, I truly knew I was still hurting from what they did to me though I tried not to acknowledge it.

Forgiveness requires you face the truth of what happened to you without discrediting the depth of what happened to you. Thanks to the help of counseling, I was able to see that I could forgive others and still acknowledge the horrible nature of what that other person did to me. I used to forgive others and say "I forgive them" while trying to make excuses for why they did what they did. It would sound like this: "I know they gossiped about me, but they were just jealous teenagers who were struggling with their own insecurities. And because of that, I can forgive them." But my counselor taught me a very powerful lesson. It's okay to say that what that person did to me was trash while still choosing to forgive. My forgiveness should instead look like this: "They intentionally gossiped about me and spread lies about me. That was wrong, but I forgive them."

In most situations where I desperately needed to forgive others so that I could heal, I felt like they were so undeserving of my forgiveness. For example, with the men who raped me, I felt like they plotted on raping me and were cruel, insensitive, and disgusting. But holding onto the anger and pain they caused me was leaving me feeling trapped. Instead of experiencing freedom, I was weighed down by the situation. I had to choose to let go to get freedom so I could heal for real.

You will have situations where you feel like others do not deserve your forgiveness. Honestly, when someone has taken cruel, egregious actions against you, they don't deserve your forgiveness. But just because your offender does not deserve forgiveness, it does not mean that you should not forgive. Forgiving others is a way of self-cleansing and self-healing.

In American culture today, many people look to several different external outlets for healing, when the focus should be on internal healing. Many Americans have adopted practices from cultures that have been utilizing the burning of sage for spiritual cleansing for years. Let's say you adopt this practice of burning sage, but you still find yourself struggling to rid yourself of past traumas, bad experiences, or negative energies. In this case, the burning of sage for smudging had no power against your internal wounds. Your traumas and negative experiences are not going to disappear by burning sage. Rather, you will have to be intentional about facing your trauma and healing from within. This is often where forgiveness comes into play. We have to take an active role in our healing and choose to actively forgive.

Imagine your soul is a room within your body that has been collecting items for years. We'll call it the Bold Room. Instead of it becoming the beautifully decorated dream bedroom it was destined to be, over the years it has become a storage space from collecting so many things. At one point your room had furniture that was functional and space to move around, but as more experiences came along, you began to pack items tightly into your space. Though they never belonged in the room to begin with, there are photos, furniture, and even trash that you stored because they were given to you. Now your Bold Room has become packed from floor to ceiling from playing Tetris trying to figure out how to make everything fit. This powerful little room hinders your growth, and it's difficult to get inside. It's your job to sort through the junk. It's your job to go in and address every item and choose to either hold onto it or let it go. That's exactly what forgiveness is like.

Forgiveness is like you going into that Bold Room and unpacking piece by piece. Forgiveness is choosing to cleanse your soul from these traumas. That's where the journey of true healing and cleansing begins. Sorting through your stuff on your own can be very difficult, and that's why I recommend multiple things to aid in your healing journey. I'll share more on that later.

As a Christian, I personally believe that the God I serve, Jesus Christ, has the miraculous ability to heal us from the inside out. We all have Bold Rooms within us that have been so tightly packed with junk that was never meant for us and having a relationship with God will help you recover from the deep wounds packed away in those rooms. The areas where shame, guilt, and condemnation try to creep in are the areas that God helps deal with. There is no spiritual healing like the spiritual healing and cleansing you'll receive from a relationship with God. There's power in the name of Jesus, and there's power in relationship with Jesus.

While you do not have to believe what I believe now, I know what I believe because it was the thing that changed my life forever. I was this broken girl who was harboring so much pain from my childhood, teenage years, and even life after college. I never really felt like I was enough or like I was worthy of much because of my past decisions. I felt completely taken advantage of by men and betrayed by women. I never wanted to trust people again because I felt like they would hurt me. I felt completely alone in the world until God came in and switched everything up for me.

My relationship with God allowed me to face my trauma, heal, and experience His unending love for me. God's love overwhelmed me to the point of healing. It's not really something I can fully explain with words, but I just know that God is real. I spent many days journaling to God while on my knees crying out to Him. Those days were the days I was able to heal. Some days I couldn't even get words out of my mouth. Only sobs, snot, and tears. God was able to look at me and deal with all my mess and still tell me that He loved me. It was His love that did it for me.

Sometimes it can be hard to let God in or even experience the reality of His love if you've been convinced that He does not exist or is not real. I had moments in life where I questioned God's existence, but when I had an honest moment with God, everything changed. I remember stopping and saying, "God if you're real, then…" I can't even remember how I finished that sentence, but God took me on a journey of proving that He was real. He proved Himself to me and has been doing so ever since. You don't have to believe what I believe, but I invite you on a journey to ask God the bold and courageous request: "God, if you are real, then show yourself to me." God dealt with me where I was, in all my mess. My mess wasn't too much for God, and your mess won't be too much for Him either.

My healing journey started with my relationship with God, but it didn't stop there. Your Bold Room can't be unpacked in a day; you have to sort through everything, get rid of what doesn't belong, clean, dust, reposition furniture, add new items, and so much more. Unpacking what's inside of you takes time and often requires a professional.

After my experience with being raped in college, it took me another year before I started seeking out therapy and counseling for it. Therapy changed my life. It was the place where I could fully examine what was in the Bold Room and see what had been scratching up the good hardwood floors of my soul. While on my healing journey with God, I had forgiven those who had done such negative things to me like the men who raped me. However, I was still negatively impacted by these situations and didn't really know it. Seeing a licensed therapist helped me get to another level of healing, and ultimately forgiveness.

One of the exercises that my therapist made me do was to tell her the story of what happened the night I was raped in college. I didn't mind talking to her about it, and I thought it would be an easy exercise since I had already shared publicly on social media and during speaking engagements about this experience. She gave me a coloring sheet and a few colored pencils. I began to tell her the story of what happened as I colored gracefully within the lines of this coloring sheet. I was zipping my way through the story, and she stopped me. She told me to pause and acknowledge my feelings and emotions. I noticed my heart racing. She pointed out that I had been clenching the pencil harder and coloring more aggressively when I got to the part when he actually raped me. I hadn't even noticed those details, but I was shocked when she mentioned that. At that point, I was a little confused because I thought I had already dealt with forgiving him.

Going to therapy helped me expose more areas where I needed healing and take practical steps toward healing. It helped me to understand that my healing was a journey and that there were many layers to forgiveness. These were the parts of my Bold Room that were being exposed. These were the areas where I still needed to extend forgiveness daily.

It takes courage to share your past traumas with others. It takes courage to share how you're still being impacted today by the traumas of yesterday. I commend you for taking the next step, no matter where you are on the journey of healing.

Healing is a very dirty process. Just like unpacking an old, dusty storage unit, unpacking your Bold Room will cause you to have to get your hands dirty and use extra strength to move things around. After spending time in therapy, I also realized there were other areas where my past traumas were impacting my life, my mindsets, and my behaviors.

For example, specifically with my sexual trauma with rape, it caused me not to trust men. When guys were nice to me, I questioned why and what they really wanted. I wondered what their intentions were even if the situation was solely platonic. I almost always assumed that they had a negative ulterior motive. My rape forced me to view every man from the broken lens of my trauma. I became increasingly anxious when it came to interactions with men which caused me to be extremely defensive to guard myself and even push men away.

My trauma from growing up in an abusive household also shifted my lens of the world. I saw nearly every conflict as a source of potential violence, so I tended to avoid conflicts when possible. Or when faced with conflict, I fought violently. I began to believe that all conflict was bad and that it was unhealthy to have conflict. I believed that conflict led to aggression, and the only way to exist peaceably with others was to avoid conflict. That is not the truth, but I accepted it as truth because of my trauma.

Not all conflict is bad. Conflict is actually healthy, but it's the way we handle conflict that can become unhealthy. We'll talk more in chapter nine about how to deal with conflict in conversations and making the bold decision to have courageous conversations.

There are so many ways that your past traumas can be impacting you. That's why we're spending so much time on this topic. You cannot become your best self without addressing what's holding you back from becoming the highest version of yourself. Since trauma impacts us in so many ways, healing from trauma is also a major process.

The journey to healing is like peeling back the layers of an onion. When you recognize that trauma exists, you have to begin to deal with the initial thing you're able to see and the residue of the trauma. The residue of your trauma is like the dirt that surrounds the onion when it's hidden underneath the ground. When pulled from the ground, the onion must be cleansed before you can begin peeling back the layers of the onion. The same is true for what's inside of your Bold Room.

You may take the time to remove all the furniture and trash that was once in the room and follow up with repositioning your furniture to be functional, but you're not done there. There is dust that has settled on the windowsills, couch cushions, and shelves. That's the residue of your pain. To the natural eye, the room may look like it's functioning well, but if you were to glide your finger across the top of your nightstand, you will see dust that has settled. The dust is the things in your life that you still need healing from because of the impact of the trauma.

But before we get to discussing the dust that has settled, let's talk about letting go. When going through what's in your Bold Room, you will have to be intentional about everything inside of it. Each of the items you evaluate within your Bold Room represent a separate life experience that caused you trauma. They're mixed in with items that were meant to be there and some that were not. Every time you are faced with a new item, you have to make a decision to either keep it as is, restore it, or completely let it go. Every item you evaluate in your Bold Room will have the following two main things connected to it: your emotions and memories.

Each life experience that caused you trauma holds emotions that you felt in the moment. Some of these are feelings that have lingered but gone unnoticed, and others are feelings that you may be aware of. You'll also find that memories are linked to your past life experiences. Typically, those memories will be what evokes the emotions and feelings regardless of if we are aware of them or not.

When you choose to let go, you're not only choosing to let go of the people who caused you pain by forgiving them. You're also letting go of the emotions and memories that may replay in your head. For me, memories of the past caused so much anxiety. Specifically with the fear of public humiliation from high school, I panicked every time I thought about speaking or performing in front of others. It got so bad that I would break out into a nervous sweat, or my mind would go blank. But this only started after that experience during my freshman year of high school.

I hadn't always been that way. Ever since I was a young child, I had a ridiculously insane ability to remember things. I loved speaking publicly and was never afraid of large crowds. I acted in plays as a kid, and I also was chosen to be a lead speaker in a school show in the sixth grade. I was always the star of whatever show or play, and the audience always expressed how they were impressed with my ability to remember and articulate my lines from the stage. I never had stage fright in high school. I danced since I was a young girl and never forgot my steps in a routine until after that terrifying experience during homecoming.

My trauma caused me to have extreme social anxiety which was the residue from my past experiences. As I mentioned earlier, our Bold Rooms contain dust that has settled over the years, and it contains emotions and memories that impact our future behaviors.

My personal healing journey started unintentionally but it hit me like a ton of bricks when I finally faced some of the trauma I'd experienced in life. For years I did not believe that I was pretty or beautiful because of my past. I did not feel beautiful.

During the summer after college graduation, everything began to change. I began to realize that I based my view of myself and view of beauty off what others had to say about me. I cared about what others thought so much that it defined how I viewed myself.

That summer I started to have more and more encounters with God, but this time it was at events. I was spending the summer hanging out with one of my cousins and she invited me to a prophetic conference. At the time, the song "Break Every Chain" had been widely popularized by the emerging gospel artist, Tasha Cobbs. To be honest, I was only excited about attending the conference because Tasha Cobbs was going to be leading worship for that night's session. God completely wrecked my life that weekend.

I sat in on the young adult's session the next day and could barely hold back my tears. I remember the sessions were so good that in between sessions I would have to go back to my hotel room just to cry and let it all out. The Spirit of God met me there in that hotel room alone. The moment I walked into the hotel room, I felt the weight of my calling hit me like a ton of bricks. I knew that God was calling me to such a great purpose, but I had to let go of my past to move forward.

I felt so emotionally and spiritually heavy, but I felt a safe space to release. I found myself sitting there on the carpeted floor just sobbing. I had been so hurt by people and mishandled by people who were supposed to protect me. I felt so unloved and out of place, and I was carrying all of that with me, everywhere I went. As I sat there on the floor crying, I felt God's true love for me. It was so overwhelming. Though I could visibly see nothing, it felt like God's presence was tangible. The feeling was something so unexplainable, but also something that I'll never forget. The heaviness was beginning to lift off me. It felt like my soul had the space to begin releasing the pain that I'd been feeling because of those who had hurt me.

God quickly shifted the focus from others to me. I've never heard the audible voice of God, but I heard in my spirit so clearly the words, "Get up." I got clear directions from God to pick myself up off the floor and get in front of the mirror. I got those instructions, but I lingered on the floor. I knew it was something I had to do, but I was not trying to face my pain. With tears in my eyes, I reluctantly picked my feet off the ground and placed my feet in front of the full-body mirror that was in front of me. I was too afraid to look at myself in the mirror at this point, but when I finally allowed myself to lock eyes with my reflection, God told me to tell myself I was pretty.

I sat there and cried some more. It finally dawned on me that for years I was not convinced of my beauty. I was allowing others' opinions to dictate my view of myself. Though I didn't want to do it, I moved forward with the exercise, still gasping for air in between my moments of weeping. I'd stare at myself and say "I am pretty" over and over again. The more I said it, the more I cried. It was honestly the first time in my life that I had ever consciously made the decision to love myself. Not only did that moment radically change my life, but God sent me away with an assignment for the week. I was to write down everything that I loved about myself and everything that was beautiful about me.

The activity to write everything that I loved about myself was tougher than I imagined and made me cry a lot more than I expected. I started by writing down my features that I thought were beautiful and those I was learning to accept as beautiful. It started with my face, my smile, the color of my eyes, the color of my hair — all the things people had complimented me on for years. I then had to venture into exploring lovable qualities about myself that I had grown to hate. When going through my facial features, I almost skipped my nose, and it made me think. This was the first time in adulthood that I realized I had grown to dislike my nose because I was teased and called Ms. Piggy as a kid.

When journaling, I had to stop and look at myself in the mirror again and say, "my nose is beautiful". I had to continue to affirm myself until I believed what I was saying. It was a completely freeing moment and it helped me to see my face and my body as beautiful.

The activity didn't stop there. I had to dig deep to go inside and acknowledge my brilliance and amazingness. Yes, I said it, and I'm unapologetic about it now. I'm courageously confident today because there was a time when I used to be timid about my brilliance. I used to back down and act as if my brilliance and achievements would make others feel uncomfortable.

After this exercise, I ended with a long laundry list of items that I recognized as beautiful things about myself that went deeper than what the eye could see. I became convinced that I was a powerful, phenomenal woman regardless of what others had to say about me.

One of the most effective actions you can take toward your healing is to love yourself and acknowledge your brilliance. My "self-love" exercise had a major way of building my confidence and shifting my self-view and self-worth. That journey was the beginning of what helped me overcome my fear of public speaking.

While I was in my MBA program, I was one of the youngest people in the program. I found myself feeling intimidated by my peers but also wondering why the heck I decided to go for such a grand achievement much earlier than the average MBA student. I learned so much in that program, but one of my favorite parts of the program was how uncomfortable it made me.

The program was packed with tons of work and what felt like endless group projects and presentations. There were weeks when our teams would have three presentations in a week. Presentations became so frequent that we had to learn how to stop relying so much on reading from flash cards and more on the content of the presentation itself. The name of the game was: know your stuff so you don't have to rehearse flashcards.

At the time, I was still deathly afraid of speaking in front of others, but I had to push through. When getting up in front of our entire class, my heart would be racing, nervous sweat would be dripping down the back of my legs, and I would be having an internal panic attack. It got easier though because of one simple thing: confidence.

Whenever I'd thoroughly study the ins and outs of the presentation is when I felt most confident. I felt like I knew what I was talking about, and it made me feel comfortable presenting in front of the crowd. When I knew my stuff, I did not have to depend on flashcards to get me through. I was able to lean on my thorough knowledge and understanding of the topic. Confidence is the same ingredient I used to help me overcome my fear of speaking in front of others alone.

For countless years, the fear of public humiliation really hindered me from speaking in public without internal panic attacks, but I had to break free from that. The first time I ever had to take the stage alone in front of an audience as a keynote speaker was my first ever Go-Getter Conference. I had planned and hosted this conference for my brand, Epic Fab Girl. In a room full of nearly 200 women, I had to deliver a message and share my story. At this point, I knew my story backward and forward, so I owned it.

I stepped onto the stage scared as heck and still afraid of being judged, but this time was slightly different. God had taken me through a journey of loving myself, so I gave myself room to make mistakes. I had no internal meltdowns thinking about *what if I fail or say something stupid.* I was no longer so bothered by the spotlight because I loved myself, accepted God's love for me, and I was not easily bothered by the negative opinions of others. I was still scared to deliver my speech, but I was confident in myself and my ability. So even though I was filled with fear, I delivered a message that, still to this day, receives raving reviews. That speech opened the door to my career as an international speaker.

After I spoke at my own conference, I started receiving invitations to speak on stages across the United States. The more I spoke, the less scary it became, and the more grace I extended myself to not need to be perfect. Not only did I speak for conferences, events, and for universities, I was even invited to preach and speak at churches. I was able to overcome my fear of speaking publicly simply because I made the decision to heal from my past. Fear is normal and it arises pretty much every time I speak publicly, but I don't allow my fear of what others have to say to allow me to crumble. I've healed from my past and become the version of myself that can exist in my Promised Land.

The same goes for you. No matter what traumas you've experienced, healing from within can really allow you to break free from fear. We already discussed how many of the fears we possess come from fear of others' opinions and fear of rejection. If you heal your inner being and love yourself fully, you can begin to thrive and not be as negatively impacted by the opinions of others. At that point, you can understand that even if others reject you or speak negatively about you, you are still a phenomenal person that's worthy and deserving of everything the Promised Land has to offer.

First comes trauma, then comes healing. To properly heal, you must understand how the trauma has impacted various areas of your life. I believe there are several layers to how traumas impact the average person, which include:

1. What and how we think

2. Our personality

3. How we treat ourselves

4. How we treat other people

5. Our behaviors

## How Trauma Impacts What and How We Think

When we go through traumatic experiences, they often impact what we think about the world around us and about ourselves. In short, it shifts our worldview and our self-view. Instead of seeing everything through a lens of truth, we view ourselves and the world through a dingy, scratched, and broken lens. Sure, maybe people have come along the journey to help you clear your blurred lens, but that doesn't always fully shift how you currently view the world.

Maybe as a part of a traumatic upbringing, your caregivers typically focused on the negative instead of the positive. Not only did they not focus on the negative things about the world, but they focused on negative things about you. Growing up in a home like that can cause trauma because it impacts the way that you view yourself and the world, through a lens of negativity instead of positivity.

Our life experiences shift us and our views in some way. For example, throughout college I believed that women were catty, jealous, and negative. I believed that women always found a way to tear each other down, compare themselves to each other, and belittle one another. I thought all women were this way, though I did not think that I was catty, jealous, and negative.

The truth is: all women are not catty. All women are not jealous and negative. I was viewing the world from a dingy lens. I was allowing my trauma with women to impact my view of women and ultimately overgeneralize the behaviors of some women to the behaviors of all. In this case, my trauma was the thing shifting my thinking in an effort to protect myself from potential hurt that may come from being in friendships with other women. Here's the truth: Just like I was not catty, jealous, and negative, there were other women like me who existed in the world, too. But for some reason, my brain could not even comprehend that truth because my trauma had my brain so focused on the bad experiences with women.

Trauma has also impacted your thought-life. But don't feel bad. You are not alone, my friend. Everything we believe about the world is not true. Some of the things we believe about the world are completely false, but we recognize them as truth because our trauma is speaking louder than anything else.

The crazy thing is that your trauma can speak to your thought life in major ways but also very subtle ways. There may be areas of your life that you never thought were impacted by your past pains, but chances are you have some digging to do, my friend.

## How Trauma Impacts Our Personality

Our personality is defined by Google Dictionary as "the combination of characteristics or qualities that form an individual's distinctive character."

What if some of the things that have become distinctive to your character and personality were never supposed to be a part of your personhood? What if some of the characteristics and traits you carry are just common responses you've developed based on your traumatic experiences?

I believe that trauma can shift us from the inside out. Once trauma shifts the way we see ourselves and the way we see the world, it can shift our nature and personality.

Let's say you've dealt with rejection often in your life, so to avoid rejection, you've become less bold in your approach to life. So instead of walking into a room with the bubbly personality you have, you hold your true personality back, bite your tongue, and flow with the energy of the people in the room for fear of being rejected. You go out of your way to shift what you say, your body language, and even how you laugh just to be more digestible. You don't want to stick out like a sore thumb.

Over the years you've become accustomed to shifting yourself in this way, so it becomes second nature to you. Is that timid, less enthusiastic version of yourself the real one? Do you feel like you can be your true self anywhere? Chances are, if you're shifting yourself consistently or don't feel you can truly be yourself anywhere you go, that may be a sign that trauma has shifted your personality.

When you recognize that trauma has shifted your personality, you have to do the work of recovering it to its original intended state. It's almost like you have to take on the role of an archeologist, excavating what was originally there and not what settled in over time. It's not easy, it takes work, but it's worth it.

I personally dealt with a ton of social anxiety simply because there was always pressure on me to be perfect. Not only that, but I'd been made fun of so much as a kid for the way that I spoke. People literally used to call me an "Oreo". If you don't know what that means, it's a mean phrase used to describe a black person who others believe "act or sound white". So, for fear of being rejected by others, I'd often choose to be quiet and shy when meeting new people. I did not feel comfortable being my full self and my fear of being judged simply turned into pure awkwardness. So, my past traumas really impacted the way I approached others and my character.

There were also times when my trauma impacted my character. After a while, I'd become so defensive by trying my best to protect myself from others. Playing sick and going to the nurse to be picked up from school got old quick. I couldn't try to avoid the teasing in high school that way, so I had to shift myself to protect myself. I had moments where I would be really mean as a high schooler. I don't really remember a ton of things I did and said to others, but there were times when I was mean. It was almost like I wanted to reject others before they could reject me simply because I wanted to defend myself from ultimately being hurt by them. I grew to have tendencies that were mean, snappy, and sometimes downright rude. I was nice to some people and mean to others if I felt like they had the potential to be mean to me. While I'm glad I grew out of that phase, it took some healing, forgiveness, and intentionality to change those ways.

As I got older, I realized that kindness was the best approach to life. I always desired to be a kind person because that's who I was deep down, but I had to protect myself and developed a hard exterior because of it.

I've had to learn how to get back to myself and rediscover my true personality that was hidden underneath all those layers of hurt and pain. Not only was I an outgoing, encouraging person, but I was extremely kind, loving, and giving. I had to learn that I was really a person that loved others deeply and extended grace often. I've learned not to respond to others' negativity and harsh words with negativity. I don't fight fire with more fire, instead I lead with love.

This is one of the major ways that I changed after surrendering my life to God. I went from being harsh in my response to others to being softer, more forgiving, and leading with love even if the other person did not treat me that way. I had to make the decision to no longer allow external factors to shift who I was as a person.

Evolving into my true personality has had a major impact on my role as a leader and as a CEO. Your character is a big deal as a leader and expert. Of course, people will say things that may be harsh, mean, or even not true about you. However, learning to be your true self regardless, instead of being reactive to negativity, can save you a lot of trouble. As we mentioned before, people are going to talk regardless. It's your job to continue to be yourself and move with honor, wisdom, and nobility.

We all know that poor character, bad judgment, and insensitivity can lead you into major mishaps in society and can cause harm and trauma to others. If you really want to position yourself as a trusted expert, you have to become trustworthy. Those who truly become trustworthy are those who move in integrity and do what is right regardless of who's watching.

You never want to be the person who, because of trauma, has a tendency to cause harm to others simply by your presence.

Nobody likes that. Experts that desire to position themselves as leaders who stand the test of time should work on their character before anything else because it can cause you harm in the long run if you don't fix it.

There are countless celebrities who rose to fame and quickly received backlash when their unpleasant personalities reached the spotlight. I believe that had these celebrities gotten healing and done the work to discover their true personality and identity, they may not have caused so much harm to those around them and their audiences. Without naming a famous person, we can all think of someone who is in the spotlight and shares unpopular opinions that are harmful to others' wellbeing.

It's increasingly important, especially as you journey to your Promised Land that you deal with the version of you that you were never meant to be. Remember, what happened to you was not your fault, but it becomes your responsibility to deal with the pieces and choose to move forward and make progress.

## How Trauma Impacts How We Treat Ourselves

There are aspects of your nature that were deeply impacted by your childhood upbringing along with the traumas you have experienced. Not only does trauma affect our personality and our tendencies, but it impacts how we treat ourselves.

I want to challenge you to read this section objectively and focus on yourself. Don't focus on how this can help someone you know. Focus on you being intentional about examining how you treat yourself. Only you and God know your thoughts. Only you two truly know how you treat yourself in every situation.

Maybe others were hard on you all your life so you're extremely critical of yourself. Maybe you were called dumb your entire life or within a traumatic relationship, so now when you make a mistake you find yourself saying things like "that was stupid" or "I'm such a fool for letting that happen".

Whatever your personal experiences have been, my question to you then becomes this: who treated you like that? Who told you that you were stupid? Who said those words to you? It's not a rhetorical question, really, who hurt you?

A lot of times we take on the same perspective of ourselves that other people have had of us. Though we may try to protect ourselves from their negativity or view of us, ultimately, we may end up treating ourselves poorly because of how others have rejected us. For example, let's say for years, like me, you were called "fat". In defense of yourself you respond in various ways like saying, "I'm not fat" or saying, "I'm beautiful" and acting like you don't care. Now this may not be every person's experience, but it was mine. I defended myself against others when they tore me down, but I was also secretly tearing myself apart privately.

Privately I'd say things like, "I'm fat" or "I'm being fat". I became obsessed with how much I weighed in comparison to others. I'd even stare at myself in the mirror and pick myself apart saying things like, "If only I could get rid of my stomach, I'd be good." I'd started treating myself the way others treated me because my view of myself had become warped based on the opinions of others. Our view of ourselves and the world impacts how we view ourselves and treat ourselves.

If you ever find yourself saying things like:

- I'm such an idiot! I don't know why I did that
- I made the dumb decision to...
- That just wasn't good enough

Trust me you're not alone. For me, the struggle was not just with my physical appearance, but it was also within how I handled myself when I made mistakes. For years, I held myself to an unrealistic expectation of perfection. I wanted to get things right in school, at work, and pretty much when approaching anything. I held this unrealistic expectation for myself because of the pressure to perform as a child. I'd always been rewarded for my achievements and accolades. I wanted to maintain how it felt to avoid rejection in that area, so I found myself working so hard to make sure I didn't fail at being perfect. When I got something wrong or made a mistake, I'd often be super hard on myself. Or if I got something wrong, made a mistake and needed help, sometimes I wouldn't ask for help simply because I wanted to appear like I had it all together. I didn't want others to think I was not smart enough or incompetent because I was asking for help.

In both situations I suffered and treated myself poorly because of it. Not only was I speaking down to myself when I made mistakes, but I was also forcing myself to suffer for my mistakes by not asking for help. I'd verbally talk down to myself at times, but I'd also mull over mistakes I made for much longer than I needed to. I'd rehearse my poor decisions in my head and wish that I'd never made that mistake. I simply did not allow myself the grace to be human and make mistakes. A lot of that was also because I did not want to upset others or let them down, which leads me to another area that you, too, may be struggling with: people pleasing.

People pleasing is extremely performative. As a black woman who studied mechanical engineering, a white-male-dominated field, I surely know the art of performance. I always had to go the extra mile in college to outperform so that I looked like I had it all together. Most days I felt like I didn't belong in those classes though I could keep up with the coursework. I really only completed my undergraduate degree because I wanted to prove to myself and the world that I was smart enough and would not give up. It was almost like a trophy for me. I refused to switch my major (though I hated it) because I did not want to appear to anyone as a failure, though it was one of the hardest things I had to do. Of course, the coursework challenged me and I learned to love the art of problem-solving, but I was not happy with the path I chose.

I tell this story to say that I'd become so performative that I'd put my own desires and sanity on the back burner. I didn't treat myself that well during that season of my life simply because I valued achievement over my sanity and mental health.

People pleasing didn't just happen with my collegiate studies. It also happened with my relationships. I often cared more about others' peace than I cared about my own. I cared about making sure everyone else was happy and pleased though

I was suffering. Whether the relationships were platonic, familial, or romantic, I'd always end up facing the problem of people-pleasing. I didn't want to have hard conversations for fear of making others uncomfortable. The irony is that I was making myself extremely uncomfortable by not having the conversations.

When you're a recovering people-pleaser like me, you have to let go of the fear of what other people will have to say about you or how they will respond to you. Despite popular opinion, our lives are more than our achievements and what others think about us. Phenomenal women, like USA Gymnast Simone Biles, made an exemplary display of this in the 2021 Olympics by choosing her mental peace over her chance to perform and compete for the medal. Every time you choose others' happiness and wellbeing over your own, you're putting your sanity at stake and sacrificing it.

To be the *Bold & Courageous* authority you were called to be, the world needs you to treat yourself well — in front and out of the spotlight.

Chances are, you may have recognized that you've been holding yourself to an unrealistic expectation of perfection. You may be treating yourself the way that others have been treating you. But now is the time for you to put those things behind you and move forward with intention so that you can truly heal and become the highest version of yourself.

After realizing that you may not have been that nice to yourself, now you have to take account of the words that you've spoken over yourself. Every word that you speak out of your mouth has power, my friend. Words speak life but they also can speak negativity. We know this because we have all had someone say something to us that has hit us like a dagger to the gut. Despite the childhood song many of us learned as kids, "Sticks and stones may break my bones, but words will never hurt me," negative words cut deeply. Negative words are a blow to our identity and future, whether they've been spoken by others or come out of our own mouths.

The Bible says in Proverbs 18:21 AMP:

> "Death and life are in the power of the tongue, And those who love it and indulge it will eat its fruit and bear the consequences of their words."

What comes out of our mouth is extremely powerful. If what we say has the power to bring life or death, imagine the weight of our words when we are speaking carelessly. You may not think much of saying things to yourself like, "I'm dumb" or "I'm fat" or "That was stupid".

Imagine that your words have the ability to trigger a fully loaded gun. Only you control what comes out of it. Bullets of negativity or bullets of positivity. The same magnitude of negativity that is thrusted out of the weapon is the same magnitude of positivity that could explode out of it. When you speak negative things over yourself, you're not only speaking word curses to your life and future, but you're also triggering a fully loaded gun. Everything around you has to respond to your words in some way.

The more you speak negativity over yourself, the more your brain registers the words you speak. You may think that you can manage saying negative things like "that was so stupid" because maybe you "didn't really mean it," but your body, your mind, and the universe takes notice.

You must learn to start treating yourself better. Be kind to yourself. Speak life to yourself. Speak truth about yourself. Give yourself grace. When you find yourself saying negative things about yourself, correct yourself.

Shifting the way you treat yourself is all a part of the healing journey. The more you heal from the wounds of others, the more you'll be able to truly heal.

Our trauma impacts how we treat ourselves, but also how we treat others which is something we need to hold ourselves accountable for.

## How Trauma Impacts How We Treat Others

When you are unhealed, you may treat others based on your trauma. How you treat others can lead to unhealthy or abusive interactions.

Past trauma may have caused you to go down the slippery slope of treating others the way you treat yourself — or the way others have treated you. You didn't like how they treated you, so in turn you take it out on the rest of the world? That doesn't make much sense, friend. While that may not be the case for everyone, it happens often.

Maybe you're the one who has been verbally, emotionally, or physically abusive to others. We are going to start to focus on how you can explore your treatment of others and ultimately get better at how you treat others. This book is not to point blame, rather, it's to allow you to take accountability so you can heal.

Now you may be reading this thinking, Candace, I have never been verbally, emotionally, or physically abusive to others. That's totally fine. We won't focus this section completely on that, but we will focus in on how exactly you may have treated others in a way that was unhealthy to both yourself and them.

To heal and become the best version of yourself, you must take accountability. You have to start with taking inventory of your relationships to understand which relationships you've developed unhealthy interactions with others. You may have found yourself raising your voice at someone, physically hitting, or touching someone inappropriately, speaking condescendingly toward them, or even neglecting or ghosting them. All of these are signs that you need healing, so your job is to become more self-aware, identify the problems, and improve your future behaviors.

I encourage you to review your family relationships, romantic relationships, work relationships, and any other relationships from the past or present to identify areas where you could have treated others better. It may be a tough pill to swallow, but it's one worth paying attention to because you can't prosper in your Promised Land while simultaneously treating others poorly. It will catch up with you if you don't check this now. The last thing you'll want to have to do is defend your reputation because of how you chose to treat other people poorly and live with the impact of those poor decisions.

Examine how you treat other people regardless of how you're feeling. Explore how you treat others when you're happy versus when you're not in the best mood. Do you treat others with respect regardless of how you're feeling, or do you allow yourself to treat others poorly when you're not feeling your best? It takes guts to be honest with yourself on this one. Real guts. So do the work and figure it out so that you don't sabotage your own success in the Promised Land.

Another major way that your traumas can impact how you treat others is by allowing others to take advantage of you. If your trauma has convinced you that you should not speak up for yourself, that your voice doesn't matter, or that you need to suffer so that others can be happy, you may find yourself struggling with being taken advantage of. It can start with the little things like saying "yes" when you really want to say "no". It could look like continuously giving someone a ride in your car who never asks to chip in on gas money though you'd like gas money. It could also look like allowing someone to move into your home temporarily because they have nowhere else to go though it's not a great idea for you at the time. It could look like allowing that same person to stay in your home though they've overstayed their welcome.

Sometimes we say "yes" to things because we don't want to feel bad for it or look bad in the other person's eyes. In the end, we typically suffer and become resentful for being nice. We should have said "no" but because we didn't, we are left to feel completely taken advantage of. You've wanted to keep other people happy and in turn you're sacrificing your own peace and happiness by not speaking up for yourself. We'll talk more about that later in this chapter, but your goal is to spot the problems so you can begin to protect your peace in your Promised Land.

Ultimately, our unhealed traumas impact how we treat ourselves and others. Many of the behaviors we have are second nature because we have been conditioned to respond that way and they have gone unchecked for years. Now, we'll pivot to focus on how our trauma impacts our actions and behaviors.

## How Trauma Impacts our Behaviors

Our experiences with trauma may impact our behaviors based on our views of the world, ourselves, and other people. There are four Promise-Land-hindering areas we will explore that are impacted by our behaviors based on trauma:

1. We don't speak up for ourselves
2. We don't take action
3. We apologize when it's not needed
4. We gossip about others

### 1. We don't speak up for ourselves.

One of the most damaging things we can do is not speak up for ourselves. It's one of the main areas that I believe hinders women, especially, in progressing into the fullness of their calling and God's promises.

When I was a kid, I grew up in an environment where my voice was often silenced. I have been and always will be a very opinionated person. I speak my mind and always have thoughts on different matters. As a kid, this was not seen as a positive thing — especially from adults. I'd often hear adults around me saying things like, "Hush, you don't have an opinion," or "Your opinion doesn't matter. Nobody asked you what you wanted."

After years of hearing that same thing, you become conditioned to keep quiet. I can point back to many times in my adolescent and adult years when I remained silent in moments when I had something to say. There was often this internal war of whether or not to speak up, or I wouldn't even speak up in a moment and regret it later. I believe I subconsciously developed a belief that my voice did not matter and that my voice would disappoint others.

I chose to remain silent or to soften the weight of my words to remain as peaceable as possible with others. I did not want to be the source of tension for anyone else. The craziest thing about that was though I didn't want to bring tension to a situation, I left the tension within me because that didn't change the fact that I still felt how I was feeling. The tension didn't disappear. By trying to protect myself by not speaking up, I caused even greater damage in the long run.

The version of me that my Promised Land deserves is the version that speaks up for herself and others. Same goes for you. Your traumas may try to convince you otherwise, but you deserve to speak up for yourself even when it's difficult.

When I was raped in college, I chose not to speak up about it at the moment. I chose not to report it to the police. From what I had learned about the guy who raped me, I knew he was a young, black professional who had a very promising career. Though part of me wanted to report it to the police, I didn't want to ruin his career. All I could think about was how there aren't that many black men that make it into college, finish college, and land great corporate jobs. I convinced myself that speaking up wasn't worth his career being impacted. As much as I wish I could go back and change my thoughts, this is my real, raw truth. I had diminished myself, my career, and my well-being in comparison to his, and I wasn't the one who was at fault.

I didn't speak up and I've spent many years reflecting on why I didn't. It's because I hadn't taken the time to heal from my past traumas. I hadn't taken the time to shift my mindset about who I am, who I'm called to be, and how significant my life, existence, and voice are. My trauma from being told to stay quiet and even from witnessing domestic abuse all contributed to my silence. My past experiences with men and insecurities contributed to my thoughts of worthlessness. I did not feel valued enough to speak up.

When I experienced sexual assault later in life, I was a new woman. I had become more convinced of my value and the significance of my voice. I made the tough decision to report the man who raped me to the police. This time I was grateful for my voice. When detectives were placed on my case, I was told that though it may be difficult to prove rape in court, even if a judge does not side with me, my assaulter's name would still be listed as a suspect in a sexual assault case. Of course, this was disheartening to hear, but I was grateful to know that speaking up made a difference. This means that if he ever violates another person and is reported, it may help the future case in some way. Either way, speaking up made a difference for me personally because I stood firm on the fact that I mattered enough to speak up for myself and to fight back in a tough situation.

This is proof that your decisions can change and so can your behaviors. It's not too late to recover your view of yourself and change your response when faced with difficult situations.

Not only did I suffer from not speaking up in my personal life, but I found that this also trickled over into my work life. While working in corporate America, there were times I didn't understand something and had more questions. There were many moments when I didn't speak up because I didn't want to cause the team to slow down with all my questions.

I'm the type of person that seriously appreciates having clarity and being able to get every possible question answered. However, there were times when I was in professional environments that made me feel like I didn't deserve the space to speak up. Sometimes it was that I was intimidated by the others in the room and other times I wanted to appear very smart and as if I knew everything. That didn't get me very far. I had to learn to speak up and ask the necessary questions to do a great job with the resources I had.

For you, there may be several areas of your life where you've chosen to remain silent or to hold yourself back for fear of being judged or because you didn't believe you were valuable enough. I challenge you to explore those areas, because I can promise you, you are suffering when you choose not to speak up.

Speaking up for yourself requires boldness, courage, and audacity. Remember that when you choose to speak up, you're still protected by the God of heaven's armies. You're backed by the Prince of Peace. Remember that your voice has immense power and deserves to be heard.

## 2. We do not take action.

Behavior inaction is a form of self-sabotage. We find ourselves settling and not going for what we really desire because our view of the world has been shaped improperly.

A lot of the women I coach in business struggle to see their expertise. It's not that they don't know they're good at what they do. That's never the problem. The problem that hinders them from walking in their greatness is always their view of themselves and their view of the world. Oftentimes these women see themselves as small and see the world as a world of impossibilities. Before working with me, they tend to diminish their power and significance in the world, not because they don't think they're gifted but because they think that they won't be able to be a big fish in the world.

As a business coach to women who helps women earn six figures a year and beyond in business, I know that sometimes self-sabotage and the wrong mentality can keep them from achieving their greatest potential. I've seen it all. Sometimes these women will assume the worst and will not apply themselves or they will assume they won't be received well when they begin posting on social media, so they give up prematurely. Not every woman is like that, but I see it often. Each of these women has to make a decision to either take action or sit back in a zone of discomfort that will get them nowhere. It'll leave them where they were before.

The women who have the most success in working with me are the ones who are able to move beyond their trauma responses and make decisions that align with their Promised Land. They don't just speak and believe that they deserve to build a six-figure business, but their behaviors align with it. Those are the clients who are able to earn nearly $300,000 in twelve months of working with me or closing six figure corporate contracts — the women who make a decision to behave based on what they believe.

The way trauma impacts your behaviors may show up in other ways, too. Let's say, for example, you've always had a dream of being an actor in Hollywood. However, your trauma has convinced you that people like you never get to build a career in Hollywood. So, because of your skewed view of the world and because you choose to diminish your own value, you choose not to pursue a career in acting. Or let's say you take it a step further and decide to enroll in acting school, but you still refuse to audition for positions because you believe that people like you will never make it into the industry. So, despite the fact that everyone around you is convinced that you'll be a phenomenal actor, you say "no" to auditions. You are sabotaging yourself based on your traumas and views of the world.

Your behaviors and actions are essential to your success and journey into the Promised Land. You can't say that you want to pursue something but become afraid in the face of it because you don't think you're good enough. At some point you have to reposition yourself to align with your power and take actions that will get you closer to your Promised Land.

These previous examples show that trauma can cause you to avoid certain actions in an effort to avoid unpleasant outcomes. Our traumas can impact what we choose to do, what we take action on, and what we choose not to take action on.

### 3. Unnecessary Apologies

Our traumas may even bring us to a place of apologizing in moments that need no apology. We say sorry to keep people happy and to dull our shine. We say sorry if we offend others though we knew what we said needed to be said. We feel guilt for our achievements, or, even worse, guilty for celebrating our achievements.

Now lean in as I say this next part and repeat after me: "I will not apologize when it's not necessary."

Do you ever find yourself saying, "I'm sorry," all the time? Do you find yourself apologizing every time you make a mistake? Chances are you're doing too much, friend. Mistakes are normal and expected in life. Especially the unintentional mistakes. If you ask me, saying, "Sorry, I didn't mean to," is code for, "I didn't want you to see my mistake and view me as less than perfect." Ouch. I know it hurts, but it's the truth. Oftentimes, the reason you're really saying sorry in moments like this is because you don't want that person to view you as not good enough. While you may be genuinely apologetic that something you did caused them harm, discomfort, or hassle, that "sorry" blurting from your mouth is all about protecting yourself from their opinion.

Let's face it. We all make mistakes. If someone views you as "less than" because you made an unintentional mistake, then that's a reflection on them and not you. You're human and nobody is perfect. Somehow, you place that expectation on yourself. But here's the truth. Most people know you're phenomenal, so one little mistake will not shift their view of you much.

Maybe your trauma has caused you to see yourself in the wrong all the time. Or maybe it has caused you to blame yourself all the time. Either way, you have to dismantle that thought pattern. You are not to blame for everything, and honestly, the world doesn't revolve around you. So, every mishap is not a reflection of you. There are often so many other factors outside of your control.

Stop apologizing when you don't need to. Period. If you're late for an important meeting, forget to do something important, or make a seriously major error, of course you're going to apologize. But don't apologize for random things that happen that are not intentional nor outside of your control.

Apologizing constantly shifts your mindset to accept blame in situations you're not to blame for. Let's take this unapologetic lifestyle a little deeper. Have you ever been told that you're too much? Too extra? Too loud? Too opinionated?

Too forward? Think you're too good? Dress too fancy? Dance too hard? Think too deeply? Take things too seriously? Overanalyze everything? The list could go on and on.

Hearing things like this your entire life sometimes forces you to believe them as truth. It forces you to shrink back instead of standing tall. Remember we said that the best version of you is the one that exists freely and has the freedom to express your individuality, uniqueness, and personal truth? If you find yourself shifting or apologizing for how you show up, it's a sign that you're living life apologetically. Please stop it. Please take time to act exactly as you desire to behave (as long as it's not seriously harmful to others).

If you catch yourself thinking that you don't want to do something or say something because you don't want to be seen as "fill in the blank," just notice it. Once you start noticing it and becoming more aware of it, you can begin to change your actions. When those thoughts arise, you will always have a decision to make. You can choose to be yourself or not to be, it's just that simple.

## 4. We gossip about others.

You may be wondering what the heck gossiping has to do with our trauma, but I'm going to share with you my theories on why we gossip and how to do better and be better.

Everyone is guilty of gossiping at some point or another. I've been guilty of it, but I've learned how to cut off or shift conversations involving gossip. Let me first define what gossip is in my book and then we'll compare it to what the dictionary says.

I believe gossip is:

1. Talking about other people and sharing someone's private information that you know to be true.

2. Sharing information that you don't know to be certain.

3. Sharing second-hand information that wasn't your information to be shared to begin with.

4. Talking about others and sharing more than just facts, rather sharing opinions that are not positive.

Google Dictionary defines gossip as "casual or unconstrained conversation or reports about other people, typically involving details that are not confirmed as being true."

Sure, gossip can be positive, but we all know it has a connotation of being very negative. I've learned a lot about gossip by examining relationships I've had with heavy gossipers and even people who mean very well but end up gossiping. I don't believe everyone gossips for the same reasons, but I do believe that these are some of the main reasons people gossip. I also believe that many people gossip without really being aware of why they're even gossiping to begin with. A lot of it is internal and requires work to shift those behaviors.

I personally believe that one of the main reasons people may gossip is because of their own insecurities. They're interested in diminishing the other person's value to be viewed as more significant and important than the person of focus in their own minds. If they can find something negative to say about someone who's successful, brilliant, or beautiful, it can often make them feel better about themselves. Feeling like they can have something to hold over another person can help them internally feel better about themselves. In situations like these, they may also be going on a campaign to diminish the other person's value in others' eyes. I believe people gossip or talk about others because they want to be seen as better or more significant than the person being gossiped about, hoping that the person listening will view them as more significant.

Now this next group of people are ones who gossip, not only because they are insecure and often intimidated by the person of focus, but because they are jealous. Jealous gossipers really wish they could have something that the person they're gossiping about has. Maybe it's that they covet the job, life, body, courage, growth, relationships, or any other things in that person's life. They feel that this person's existence threatens their ability to succeed, and they're upset about it. This type of gossiper is dangerous because most people don't even realize they're jealous when they are jealous. They just feel some sort of tension within themselves that they cannot explain, and they allow that energy to turn into things like gossip or negative behaviors.

Some folks gossip because they have been hurt by the person they're gossiping about. They gossip because they've learned information about this person that would alter others' view of them. In an effort to get others to view them negatively, they gossip so that others can shift their view of this person. These types of gossipers do it out of resentment and revenge.

Some people just gossip because they have nothing better to do and nothing to celebrate in their own lives. I believe that people like this are really discontent with their own lives, so they have nothing better to focus on other than talking about others. People like this who gossip are dangerous because they are miserable, and we know that misery loves company.

Then there is the group of people who gossip because they are prideful. This group of people genuinely believe they are better than other people. They use gossip as a weapon to stay on top in their minds and to be viewed by themselves and others as better than those they gossip about. They tear down others for the sake of trying to keep themselves on top. Their pride causes them to, blindly and negatively, speak about others in an effort to stroke their ego.

Whew. Gossip is an ugly beast. It has the ability to snatch your Promised Land and hinder you from walking fully into it. It can cause you to lose friends, relationships, and even sabotage your own success. Gossip isn't worth your future. You have enough to fight for into the Promised Land, and you don't want to be bringing on more unnecessary battles just because you cannot control your mouth.

Even if you gossip unintentionally, sometimes others may not have the best intentions and will spread that information to try to diminish your character. The important thing here is to understand that every conversation isn't meant to be discussed with everyone.

It takes serious courage to look yourself in the mirror and be honest about the fact that you gossip and why you gossip.

Of course, this book is not to make you feel terrible about yourself, rather it's meant to help you do better and learn how to shift into the person God called you to be. It takes a lot to control your own tongue, especially when you're trying to transition from gossiping.

> Matthew 12:34 ESV says, "Out of the abundance of the heart the mouth speaks." This is evidence that people gossip because of what's in their hearts. Whether you gossip out of pride, idleness, discontent with your own life, jealousy, or insecurity, it's an indication that you need healing and your heart needs recovery. What does this mean for you? It means that you should position yourself to become pure in heart. When you shift yourself to allow God to purify your heart, you'll be able to make room for the version of you that you were destined to be.

Gossip can literally ruin you. There are several verses in the Bible that support this truth:

> Proverbs 13:3 NIV says, "Those who guard their lips reserve their lives, but those who speak rashly will come to ruin."

> 1 Peter 3:1 ESV says, "For 'Whoever desires to love life and see good days, let him keep his tongue from evil and his lips from speaking deceit;"

> Matthew 15:18 ESV says, "But what comes out of the mouth proceeds from the heart, and this defiles a person."

The craziest thing about gossip is that after life on earth is complete, the Bible states in Matthew 12:36-37 ESV, "I tell you, on the day of judgment people will give account for every careless word they speak, for by your words you will be justified, and by your words you will be condemned." We will have to give account for every single word we have ever spoken, and, as Christians, I know that is a huge wake-up call for many of us.

If you truly want to be the version of you that your future requires, you will have to intentionally stop being a gossiper. It may not be easy, but it requires effort. You have to make the decision to heal from whatever has been causing you to gossip and also consciously make the commitment not to gossip.

For you, shifting away from gossiping may mean that certain relationships in your life have to end. If that's the case, pray that God gives you discernment about what to speak on and what not to speak about in your relationships.

Living a life with minimal gossip will have its benefits. It will help you avoid drama and stay focused on what God called you to do. Regardless of the reason you gossip, it's your job to take accountability for your actions and begin to heal.

## Healing from Your Pain

While the trauma you experienced was not your fault, your healing is your responsibility. Time does not heal everything; instead, time makes more room for you to suppress your true pain. Healing from your pain requires intentionality.

While I'm no professional, I'm going to share steps that have helped me heal from the trauma and pain I've experienced over the years.

## Steps to Healing from Trauma

1. **Identify what you need to heal from.** The first step in the process is to get real with yourself and pay attention to what you need healing from. Consider your life experiences and the moments that made you feel less than enough or that caused you distress. Once you identify what you need to heal from, it'll be easier to address it.

2. **Assess how your trauma has impacted you.** With your trauma in mind, ask yourself how it has impacted your thoughts, personality, actions, decision-making, and your treatment of yourself and others. I personally believe trauma impacts everything — in both big and subtle ways. It's important to do some digging with your behaviors to see what really has caused you to react to the world that way. Sometimes you may find that you recognize the impact of the trauma before you identify what caused you to behave this way. It's important to do the work regardless

3. **Create a healing plan and do the work.** By now you know that it's important to take your healing into your own hands. One of the best ways to do that is to be intentional and create a plan for healing. However, it's not enough to simply create a plan, rather you have to do the work. Creating a plan to heal will help you make progress on your healing journey.

## Creating a Plan to Heal

This section is dedicated to helping you create a plan to heal from your past trauma and wounds. The crazy thing about life is that we will always be facing new situations that may bring trauma and even open old wounds. That's why I believe it's imperative to be intentional about your healing journey and develop a plan to maintain your freedom.

Your Promised Land requires the *Bold & Courageous* you. Remember the dust that settled into your Bold Room? You've got to be intentional about dealing with those things. Your Bold Room may have been cluttered with so many things like hurt, pain, regret, grief, and countless other things. As you begin or continue your healing journey, you're choosing to reorient what's in there. You're choosing to cleanse your heart and soul of the things holding you back from being the true version of you that God created you to be.

Everyone's healing journey will look different. Each of us has encountered unique experiences and we require varying levels of attention and support. I believe a healing plan that includes the following will help you tremendously on your journey to healing.

- **Professional Counseling or Therapy.** Seeking a professional for counseling or therapy is extremely important. Professionals are the most qualified and skilled individuals to help address your psychological and physiological needs. Especially if you've experienced trauma in your childhood or adult life, therapy has the potential to be extremely restorative in your journey. Not all professionals will be a perfect match for you, but I encourage you to do the work to find the right therapist who will aid in your healing process. The right therapist will help you dismantle beliefs and behaviors that are hindering you from being the best version of yourself.

- **Inner Healing and Deliverance.** Getting faith-based inner healing and deliverance is extremely important to address any demonic influence your past traumas have had on you. This is essential for breaking strongholds on your mind, body, and soul so you can flourish in your Promised Land. Deliverance doesn't have to be scary or churchy. It's simply about initiating your healing process for the deep wounds your trauma has caused you. When looking for someone who specializes in inner healing, be careful not to lean toward spiritualism or with practices like reiki or chakras as they can cause more harm than healing. Find someone who is biblically based and knowledgeable about the word of God so you can get proper healing.

- **Faith-based affirmations.** Repeating affirmations can help you shift your mindset about yourself, your future, and your expectations about your future. Using affirmations daily will help you shift into a place of recovering your view of yourself and align with what God has to say about you and your future. You can partner your desires with biblical truths that have power to shift your mindset and your life.

- **Intentional and Vulnerable Prayer.** There's so much power in praying to God and having conversations with

God that allow you to heal. Having a consistent prayer life is essential to your healing process because you can give your feelings and emotions to God and allow yourself to be vulnerable with God. I believe that the more vulnerable you are with God, the more He's able to heal you from the inside out. God desires for you to be healed, and He delights in the process of healing you.

- **Supportive Community and Covenant Relationships.** Healing happens in many parts. Having a supportive community of people will help you as you process through your pain. It's important to have covenant relationships that are God-ordained so you can trust them with your pain. Having covenant relationships with friends, peers, mentors, and family will help you remain covered in prayer while having the safe space to communicate your feelings and thoughts as you heal.

- **Church or Community of Believers.** There's nothing like coming together with other believers to stay plugged in as you heal. I highly recommend being a part of a local church beyond just attending church services. I believe this is where the best relationships are born — through community. Find ways to get active in a local church or small group to stay connected with like-minded people. Chances are, you may find people who have experienced similar struggles and are moving forward in life, as well. Even if you're not connected to a local church, you can still find other ways to connect with a community of believers. For example, my community, Epic Fab Girl hosts a weekly prayer call for Christian women entrepreneurs. While what we do at Epic Fab Girl is not a church service, it serves as a place for women to believe God and stand in faith together. Having positive, like-minded people around you on your healing journey will be refreshing and help you live the way you desire — healed and free.

• • •

Healing builds your courage. The more you heal, the more you'll have the freedom to make courageous decisions.

Learning to love myself helped me overcome the fear of speaking in public. I had to start loving myself enough to give myself permission to make mistakes.

Your healing is imperative to your future. Below you'll find an activity that I've used throughout the years to help me heal and love myself more.

Healing activity:

1. Create a list of past memories and traumatic experiences that you've experienced in your life from childhood until now.

2. Take time thinking about each individual experience and journal about the instance.

3. As you journal through each instance, answer the following questions:

    a. What do you remember about the situation?

    b. What did you feel at the time?

    c. What feelings and emotions arise now as you take time to think about the experience?

4. Now, examine how your trauma has impacted you by answering the following questions:

   a. How did you view yourself differently after this situation?

   b. How did you change after this experience?

   c. How did the way you viewed the world change after this instance?

   d. How have your traumas impacted how you think?

   e. How have your traumas impacted your personality?

   f. How have your traumas impacted your actions and behaviors?

   g. In what ways have you treated yourself poorly?

   h. In what ways have you treated others poorly?

5. Moving forward:

   a. How can you be more kind to yourself?

   b. How can you be more kind to others?

6. Look yourself in the mirror and create a list of all of the beautiful things about you and your personality.

7. Take time to sit with God in a tranquil place. Keeping your list of traumas and list of things you love about yourself in mind, ask God to heal you. Allow God to speak to you and journal what you feel, sense, or hear.

As I close out this chapter, I want you to repeat this prayer aloud with me:

*Dear God,*

*I thank you for being a healer. Only you know everything that I've ever walked through. Only you know all of the things that I've had to endure to get to this day. I pray that you would heal the areas of my heart that are broken. I pray that you would restore the areas of my identity that have been fragmented. Help me to view myself the way that you view me. Help me to trust you more with my future decisions. Thank you for keeping me. I pray that you will continue to heal and restore me so that I can walk fully, boldly, and courageously in purpose.*

*Amen.*

# 5 Bold & Courageous Decisions

One of the scariest things I've ever done was quit my job in corporate America. I was sure that God told me to quit my job that year, but I had become so dependent on that consistent paycheck and honestly, I didn't have a way to make any money outside of driving Uber and Lyft. Since I'd decided to quit my job in August of 2017, I had already drafted my letter of resignation during the summer of 2017. I drafted it but I never hit send. I was waiting until the end of August to actually quit because that was the deadline I had given myself after chatting it up with God.

I specifically planned to save an extra $15,000 by August to be able to have a cushion to quit my job. As the year flew by and August kept getting closer, my bank account started to dwindle. I went from building up a small savings balance to draining my savings. That year, I had so many unexpected experiences and emergencies come up that required me to spend my savings. It was chaotic. My basement flooded, my washing machine broke, my refrigerator broke down, and so much more. While I'd been trying to cut back on my expenses, it became quite difficult to save any money at all.

So here I was, convinced that this was my year to quit my job but there was no significant amount of money in the bank to support that. I was basically living paycheck to paycheck at that point. I couldn't understand why my money was looking so funny when I felt I heard God tell me to quit my job. For most of the year I didn't share what I was plotting with anyone except for a few very close friends.

By the summer of 2017, I landed a work project that wasn't as difficult for me. It made me feel like I could deal with corporate America for at least another year while I was on the project, but to be honest, I was completely bored with the work I was doing. I got placed on a project in the middle of Omaha, Nebraska. As a girl from the city, I did not like it, but I convinced myself I could tolerate it to pay the bills for now.

To be honest, I was still on the fence about quitting my job. My analytical nature wasn't helping me choose to quit, either. I had so many questions. How would I pay my bills? What if I went broke? What if I lost my home to foreclosure? What if I can't keep my lights on? What if I fall behind on bills? What will my life look like? I was so worried about my fear of failing that I couldn't focus on making a decision.

I then began to ask people for advice about my desire to quit my job. I am a believer of the Bible. So, one verse I kept leaning on in that season was Proverbs 11:14 ESV which says, "Where there is no guidance, a people falls, but in an abundance of counselors there is safety."

So, what did I do? I sought counsel and advice from others. I began to ask others this question: "What's the difference between having crazy faith versus walking in wisdom?" To be honest, nobody could give me a substantial answer. I sought out leaders from church, friends who I trusted, and even other business owners. I could not wrap my mind around the concept of moving in faith but being wise about my decisions. I was truly torn on the inside because I had no clue how I was going to make a decision to leave, though I knew I needed to.

Then one day I went to church and as I was sitting in the audience during a training, a prophet got on the microphone and called me out of the crowd. Here's what the word said:

> "God is going to blow upon the curriculum and ideas that you've been writing and dealing with behind the scenes. God is going to expand you and cause you to teach others these systems and strategies he has been pouring into you behind the scenes. God said this is going to be a time of greatness and He's going to give you a level of business that you have not had before."
>
> "The Lord says the enemy had come against you to dwindle or hinder what God was trying to manifest in you to cause you to break down under the weight and the pressure of what God's giving you. God said he is going to send a level of peace to your life and a level of comfort knowing that God is with you. This will be a season of great progression.
>
> God said you were waiting for him to confirm some things to you, and you have been asking the Lord, when am I going to get a word? The Lord says, I speak to you to let you know you are on my mind

and that you are my daughter and that you are one that I have had my hand on since you were a child."

That prophetic word was one of the major things that gave me courage about this decision. A lot of people asked me what really gave me the courage to take the leap of faith, and it was a combination of things.

First of all, I had to make the decision for myself; nobody else could do it for me. Not only that, one of my good friends brought it to my attention that while I was asking for advice about quitting my job from many people, I hadn't really asked anybody who had quit their job before or built a wildly successful business. He made it clear that wise counsel must be chosen well, and that was when I began to realize that God was pushing me to make a decision on my own based on what He had already spoken.

God told me it was time to quit my job, but there were so many moments I second-guessed myself. For a while I wondered if I really heard God correctly. I started to doubt my ability to hear from God clearly. Everything around me was chaotic and it didn't make sense to decide to quit my job when it did. The facts were this: I had no income and very little savings. None of it made sense.

After I heard that prophetic word, it ignited me. It affirmed that I had heard from God clearly and that it was time to make that shift. I received that prophetic word in July of 2017. At that point, I made up in my mind that God was likely going to find a way to miraculously allow $15,000 to end up in my bank account. I was confident in that, but when the end of August came around and I still didn't have the $15,000 in my bank account, I talked myself out of making the decision to quit.

There I was. Letter of resignation drafted. Confirmation from God to me personally. Prophetic word to confirm what God had already said. But I still decided not to quit. I was so scared. It was literally paralyzing. I had no idea what to do, but I felt this extremely strong pull and calling to quit, but I just couldn't do it.

In the middle of August 2017, I felt led to watch a sermon on YouTube from a well-known pastor. That sermon was one of the final straws that helped me decide to leave. Ultimately, the sermon's message was this: God is using this uncertain situation to cause you to accelerate, so stand on what God said. The pastor even said, "I know God is telling you to quit the job that was a miracle to get but trust Him." I felt like he spoke those words directly to me. I laid there in the hotel room bed staring at the ceiling, crying because nothing made sense, but I knew that this message was for me. I knew it was time to quit, but I had no idea how I was going to make it happen.

I was waiting on God to move miraculously before I quit my job, but that's not what happened. God wanted me to make a decision based off what He said and that's when everything shifted.

Thursday, August 30, 2017, came and I had not yet quit my job. I went into the office in Omaha, Nebraska and though I felt discomfort, I still tried to work through the day. I checked my email and had received an email from my career counselor saying, "Congratulations on 3 years at the firm." What he didn't know was that his email reminded me of something God had told me when I first landed that job. I remember God told me he was giving me three years at the company. I could no longer contain myself.

As I was sitting in my corner cubicle, I tried to hide my tears. It was too much to bear. I grabbed my car keys and swiftly found my way to the nearest door. I sat in my rental car and sobbed. I was so uncomfortable. I knew I didn't belong at that job anymore and I also felt a spiritual weight I'd never felt before. Here's the best way I can explain it... Though I'd never been pregnant before, it felt like I was pregnant and trying to abort a baby at nine months. It felt like it was time to push, but I was trying to abort the mission.

I gathered myself as much as I could and finished the work-day. Ironically enough, I flew home to Chicago that day and met my niece for the first time who was born that same day. I'd been crying and overwhelmed all day, but I was getting to the point that I felt like I needed to take action. I had no idea how it was going to work out.

Once I got settled at home the next day, I sat there praying to God and asking Him if it was really time to quit. I still hadn't sent the letter of resignation and I still hadn't miraculously received $15,000 in my bank account. I was scared to obey God because I wasn't sure how things would actually work out.

As I stood at the foot of my bed, I heard God tell me to revisit my budget again and check to see how much money I'd get if I quit my job. I realized that I'd receive a payout from the paid time off I hadn't used along with other money from company investments. That amount added up to exactly $15,000 and some change. I was mind blown.

Here I was waiting for God to send the $15,000 far in advance of me quitting my job, but God decided to show me my provision the same day I put in my two weeks' notice. It was almost like God was waiting for me to decide. I submitted my letter of resignation and declared that September 15, 2017, would be my last day at the firm.

Up until the moment I sent my resignation letter, I was filled with anxiety and worry. But the moment I submitted my letter of resignation, I felt an extreme peace over my mind, body, and soul.

Let me be honest, it's very scary to obey God when things don't make sense. It's scary to make a risky decision when you have no idea what the outcome is going to look like. It's scary, but that doesn't mean it shouldn't be done. I've learned that many miracles in the Bible were initiated by way of obedience to God. God gave instructions that may not have made much sense, but as the person was obedient, He delivered. For example, with the children of Israel crossing the Jordan River...

For context, this is in Joshua chapter three after the Israelites had been wandering through the wilderness for forty years and Joshua was appointed their leader to lead them into the Promised Land. According to the first chapter of Joshua, God told him to be bold and courageous and not to fear because God would be with them every step of the way.

As Joshua and the Israelites were nearing the Promised Land, they had to cross the Jordan River. God instructed Joshua and the Israelites to follow the men who were holding the ark of the covenant. God's instruction to Joshua was this: "Tell the priests who carry the ark of the covenant: 'When you reach the edge of the Jordan's waters, go and stand in the river'" (Joshua 3:8 NIV).

Let's be clear here, the Israelites would be face to face with the Jordan river with no way to get around it and God's instructions to them were to go and stand in front of the river? It's not certain how wide the river was at that time, but some historians say it was about two miles wide and swelling. Those instructions that God gave did not make much sense at all. Stand at the river? Was God going to send a boat? Was God going to make the river disappear momentarily? Was God going to create a bridge for them to cross? Was God going to miraculously transport them to the other side? Either way, Joshua did not know. All he knew was what God told Him to do and that God promised He would be with him always.

I'm going to let you read what happens next on your own, straight from the Bible in Joshua 3:15-17 NIV:

> "Now the Jordan is at flood stage all during harvest. Yet as soon as the priests who carried the ark reached the Jordan and their feet touched the water's edge, the water from upstream stopped flowing. It piled up in a heap a great distance away, at a town called Adam in the vicinity of Zarethan, while the water flowing down to the Sea of the Arabah (that is, the Dead Sea) was completely cut off. So the people crossed over opposite Jericho. The priests who carried the ark of

the covenant of the Lord stopped in the middle of the Jordan and stood on dry ground, while all Israel passed by until the whole nation had completed the crossing on dry ground."

It's estimated that about 40,000 people crossed the Jordan River that day. Not only did God hold back the waters of the Jordan River, but He provided dry ground for them to walk on. This meant that there was no mud sticking to their feet as they walked. They did not have to be miserable as they crossed the river. They had dry ground to walk on as they journeyed into their Promised Land. God allowed the Israelites to peaceably cross the Jordan River that day.

Obeying God sometimes requires you to throw all logic out the window. Logic and miracles cannot coexist. Your logic may be the thing that's stopping you from making a decision that could take you to your next level of success. Don't get so caught up in logic that you miss the miracle that God may be trying to make happen in your life.

I personally believe that God does miracles for His people regardless of if you choose to believe in Him or not. You may have given your life to God, or you may not have, but that doesn't stop God from working and moving in your life. We all have experienced some form of miracle in our lives that did not require our obedience. However, I believe that when you are on assignment, something powerful happens when you partner with God and choose to obey Him. There's another level of miracles that are unlocked when you surrender your life, your plans, and your decisions to God.

When faced with the Jordan River, Joshua had to make a decision. Was he going to lead the people into the river? Or was he going to hesitate or completely disobey? Let's be very clear that Joshua had a choice. Joshua had to make a decision. I believe the thing that we can learn from Joshua is that not only did he obey God, but he did not hesitate to obey God. He did not drag his feet. He immediately gave instructions to those who were under his leadership and moved forward with action. Joshua had to make the risky decision to lead a group of 40,000 people to a riverbank to cross it.

Imagine the type of trust in God you have to have to lead thousands of people to a swelling riverbank. Joshua's actions showed that He trusted God fully. Joshua focused on his role in the miracle, trusting that if he obeyed God, God would deliver.

I think one of the most interesting things about this story is that God gave Joshua the final outcome at the beginning of the journey. God shared His promise with Joshua at the beginning. God told Joshua that He was giving the Israelites the Promised Land, but He did not give him the play-by-play blueprint to get there. All Joshua had to depend on was his history with God while under Moses' leadership and that God would be with him. Joshua witnessed God split the Red Sea for the Israelites while under Moses' leadership. So you could imagine that his history with God made him confident in God. Joshua's job was to trust God and obey. His role was never to question how God was going to do something, rather that He would do exactly what He promised. Joshua had to hold onto the promise. Joshua had to trust God in every moment.

I believe Joshua was able to make risky decisions because he fully put his trust in God. Your life is no different. Maybe God has promised you something that you've been waiting on for years, but you must remember that God will always be with you and deliver on His promises. You cannot get to the promised land without having to make risky decisions to get you there, but it requires an unrelenting trust in God. Just like God told Joshua that He would always be with him, God will always be with you.

To get into your Promised Land, you, too, have to make risky decisions. Sometimes you have to put it all on the line without knowing how things are going to turn out. Our logic may flood our minds with questions about how things are going to work out or we may even start to doubt. But remember this: your job is not to figure out how, your job is to trust God and obey.

When I quit my job, I had no idea how things were going to work out. I just knew that God promised me success as an entrepreneur. When faced with quitting my job, I had to make a decision. I had to either choose fear or choose obedience to God. If I were to choose fear, I'd continue to exist in an uncomfortable place at my corporate job. But if I were to choose obedience to God, I was choosing a world of the unknown.

The fear of the unknown can stop you in your tracks. Knowing details often gives us comfort and security. If you're anything like me, I like to know *everything* so that I can plan appropriately. I like things in my life to flow as smoothly as possible.

However, if I wanted to get closer to my Promised Land, I had to make decisions based on obedience to God and let go of figuring out the details on my own.

It was the miraculous nature of events in my life that gave me the courage to say yes to my future even though it didn't make sense. I understood that God would be with me every step of the way, and that understanding empowered me quit my job. Was my mind flooded with questions? Yes. Was I nervous as heck? Yes. But did I trust God with my future? It was an absolute yes.

The decision must happen in your mind first before you take action on it. You have to decide. If you want to get to the place of your Promised Land, you will have to make many decisions on the journey.

Now I want you to lean into what I'm about to say next. Inaction is a decision. Choosing not to take action is actually a decision. Inaction means that you have decided in your mind that the situation will not work out in your favor. Until you **decide** to move forward toward your Promised Land, you will remain stagnant where you currently are. Thinking about it isn't enough to get you into the Promised Land.

Many of us know people who speak of life from a place of "what ifs" and regrets. There are the people who, as they grow older, reminisce on the decisions they wish they could have made. They feel like had they decided differently, their life would look different. The truth is their decisions have gotten them where they are.

Sometimes complacency is comfortable. You can remain comfortable and not be challenged where you are, but the journey to the Promised Land requires that you forsake all ideas of comfort. Your journey to your Promised Land is not about your comfort, it's about your purpose.

Let's take Joshua, for example. Joshua's decisions were impacting thousands of people. I'm going to bet that if you're reading this book your decisions can impact thousands of lives, as well. When you say no to risky decisions on your purpose journey, you're also saying no to thousands of people who are waiting on your yes.

Joshua was leading the Israelites out of a space of captivity and into a new world filled with promises. He was taking people who had been enslaved into a world of complete freedom and bliss. So, every decision he made had an impact on those people he is called to.

I challenge you not to think about the scary decisions you make while only focusing on you. I challenge you to imagine the people who you're going to help in your Promised Land. When it comes time to make a scary decision, get those people in your head and imagine as if you're either saying "yes" or "no" to them. I want you to understand that your decisions have an impact that goes way beyond just you.

Of course, when you're facing scary decisions, things in your Bold Room may start to get exposed. Fears are going to arise. It's okay, it's normal. Deal with what comes up and keep pushing forward. Your Bold Room does not have to be completely cleared out, dusted, and positioned perfectly for you to begin journeying into your Promised Land.

Let's talk about a few common bold and courageous decisions you may have to encounter on the journey to *your* Promised Land.

## Deciding to leave a romantic relationship

Sometimes one of the scariest things to do is to leave a relationship you've invested so much into. People leave relationships for many different reasons. Sometimes it's because the relationship is not healthy or has become harmful to them. Other times people may leave relationships because it's no longer serving them, or they have grown apart.

Who you choose to be romantically involved with absolutely impacts your journey into and inside of the Promised Land. Your relationships, especially romantic ones, should be conducive to your growth and ability to flourish in the Promised Land.

Deciding that you no longer want to be with someone can often take time to figure out. Making the decision to leave is always a courageous one to make, especially if the relationship is causing harm to you. As a woman who has been in an abusive relationship before, I know the level of guilt you can feel for deciding to leave a relationship.

Finding the courage to say "this relationship no longer serves me" is tough. But it's important to evaluate how this relationship has impacted you, your health, your mind, and your overall well-being. Relationships exist for more than just companionship and sex, so it's important to look beyond those aspects to evaluate if this relationship is one that's conducive to a healthy future.

Sometimes, especially as women, we can become so attached to the idea of being loved or eventually married that we convince ourselves that the relationships we are in are worth saving. We may even sacrifice everything including our sanity to have the comfort of a relationship or the stability it brings whether in security or financial stability.

Sometimes when you've been in a relationship for so long with someone, you may not be able to picture your life without that person. You may be so tied to what it looks like to be in that relationship that you're afraid to envision a world beyond it. You might even struggle with the shame of telling others it ended because you fear it may be a bad reflection of you.

But remember this: every time you stay in a relationship that no longer serves you, you are saying "no" to the people you're called to. You're also saying "no" to your Promised Land.

Sometimes, especially as Christians, we get so caught up trying to say that the devil is busy. But the devil isn't always as busy as we think. Sometimes our decisions are keeping us in a place where the devil doesn't have to do anything other than leave us right where we are at. You might be thinking that the devil is at work, but in reality, your decision to remain in an unhealthy relationship may be the thing causing so much conflict and turmoil in your life, not the devil.

Relationships are hard work, but they do not have to be harmful and difficult. There's a world of relationships that come with ease.

I challenge you to evaluate your relationship to see if you're becoming better because of it or if it's hurting you. Once you evaluate that information for yourself, it's up to you to make the decision.

## Deciding to quit your job

You may have dreams of quitting your job. You may be in a position where you are wanting to quit your job to transition to another job or you may be considering quitting your job to pursue full-time entrepreneurship. Either way, it's a bold and courageous decision to make.

Let me be clear: I don't think full-time entrepreneurship is for everybody. Everybody is not called to it. However, I believe that quitting a job is a decision that many entrepreneurs are faced with. This is another ridiculously scary thing to do, mainly because within western culture, many people depend on their jobs for financial security. Our jobs fuel much of our lifestyles including what we can do, where we're able to go and even the life and legacy we leave for our families.

But here's the thing. Job security isn't really security at all. We all know that at any point in time you can be let go from a job. We've seen it happen during the recession of 2008-2009 and we also saw massive layoffs in 2020 during the COVID-19 Pandemic. Sometimes we have been made to feel like having a paying job is all the security we need to feel financially secure. Having a job and trusting money creates a false sense of security. Our true security comes from knowing that God is a provider and that He provides for every need we have.

We have so much fear of the unknown when it comes to quitting a job. In reality, the future is always unknown and uncertain. Even if you have a "secure" job, you don't know how the future will unfold.

So, when deciding to quit your job, you will have to weigh your options. Is staying on your current job healthy for you and in alignment with where you're headed? Either way, you are going to have to make the decision. Nobody can make the decision for you.

## Deciding to leave a church

So, you know I'm here for talking about taboo topics, and, of course, if you're a Christian who has attended churches in your lifetime, you know there can be a fair share of drama and politics at any. However, that's not the focus of this section. I want to focus on making the bold and courageous decision to part ways with a church or a ministry, regardless of your reasons.

Who pours into you matters. The leadership you're under from a spiritual perspective matters, too. I personally believe that if you get to a point where you feel God is leading you to leave a church, listen and obey.

In 2017, I left a church ministry I had grown to love, where I served in leadership, and had built community. Prior to making that decision in 2017, God had been dealing with me about leaving the church for at least a year prior. I saw things that made me question a few things about the church and the integrity of its leaders, but I honestly ignored them and extended grace because I felt so connected to the vision of the ministry. I took forever to make my decision to leave because I wanted to be certain that I was hearing from God and that my decision to leave was not influenced by anybody else. By the time I decided to leave the church in 2017 I wished I'd left much sooner.

My advice about leaving a church or ministry you're connected to is this: leave if that's what God told you to do. It can be hard especially if you really loved the church, served, and were connected to the people. However, attending a church has an impact on your calling and where God is taking you. The church you're connected to has the ability to impact your journey into and through the Promised Land.

Leaving a church does not have to be a bad thing. If God is pulling you in another direction, you have to understand that God is sovereign so it's key to obey Him even if it doesn't make sense. You may have to have some difficult conversations and you may even struggle after leaving the church when you realize that those you were once connected with are not as invested in your life after you leave, but you have to obey God regardless.

It's an extremely courageous decision to leave a ministry when God says that your time there is up. Be careful to make sure that you hear from God about your decision, and when you hear from God about your decision, obey Him without hesitation.

# Deciding to let go of a client

As an entrepreneur one thing I was never really prepared for was having to discontinue a relationship with a client. There are times when your business may pivot or when your working relationship with a client needs to come to an end. Letting go of a client is a bold decision to make and a courageous decision, at that.

Ending a working relationship with a client may happen because you no longer desire to offer the services or continue a partnership with them. Either way, making that decision can be a tough one to make, but you have to do what's best for you and your business. Oftentimes, I've found that ending a working relationship with a client is also beneficial for them, too.

For example, in the beginning of 2020 I began offering done-for-you email marketing and social media management services to a well-known radio host in Chicago. We had an amazing working relationship. I did a great job at it, but after about five months of working together, I knew it was time to shift. I had so much other work on my plate at the time and I decided to discontinue my social media management services for my clients. I realized that I loved social media, but I primarily enjoyed it from a strategy and ideation perspective. I knew if I continued working with this client that the quality of the work he would get from me would not be my best effort, and I did not want to end our work relationship on bad terms. So, I decided to walk away from the opportunity.

At first, I was scared to have the conversation with him about ending the working relationship because I was running all his digital marketing efforts with email and social media. Instead of allowing fear to stop me from having the conversation, I spoke up and I'm so glad I did. My client was, to my surprise, extremely happy for me and glad to know that I was transitioning my business to focus more on coaching full-time.

There are other times when a working relationship with a client may become uncomfortable or unhealthy, and it's okay to say "no" to working with them. I've learned to speak up and make the decision quickly so that I do not linger in the relationship longer than I need to. It can be a hard decision to make, but if you do it with integrity, you will be fine.

## Deciding to let go of an employee

Sometimes you may be in a position where you are tasked with letting go of an employee or someone in your company. Yes, indeed it's a hard decision to make, but you have to be bold and courageous.

Being bold and courageous in this situation does not mean you need to be harsh or unforgiving, rather you need to be courageous in your approach. So that means that you face the situation with facts, with grace, and courageously consider the other person's perspective. It's not easy to make that decision but allowing yourself to delay without making the decision will only cause more harm than good.

Remember that when someone is a part of a team or an organization, it's not about a personal matter, rather you have to do what's best in the interests of the company and its owners.

It's not personal, so be sure to make your decision based on that and the factors that impact the owners.

When you feel fear come up, you must ask yourself what you're truly afraid of. Address it and make your decision.

## Getting to know a new person

Friendships and relationships are extremely essential to flourish in your Promised Land. Proverbs 27:17 NLT states, "As iron sharpens iron, so a friend sharpens a friend." It is good for you to have relationships that build you up, fortify you, and strengthen you.

Ecclesiastes 4:9-10 NLT states,

> "Two people are better off than one, for they can help each other succeed. If one person falls, the other can reach out and help. But someone who falls alone is in real trouble."

Let's be very clear that you need healthy friendships in your Promised Land. You do not need to be isolated on your journey. Some people say it's lonely at the top, but I personally believe that God will staff your life with the right people who love you unconditionally, understand your calling, and can be a friend to you — even at the top.

Getting to know and trust people as an adult can be difficult, especially if you've experienced being let down so much in life. Whether platonic or romantic, healthy relationships are a major part of your Promised Land. Your relationships impact the way you think, what you're influenced by, and your overall well-being and mental health. When building healthy relationships, it's important to build with people you already know, but also expand and open yourself up to new relationships.

Sometimes we may get to know people who are complete strangers to become friends with them and grow to know them personally. Other times we may get to know someone more personally after knowing them as an acquaintance or through others. Either way, getting to know a stranger is courageous and pulling an acquaintance closer into friendship is also courageous.

When meeting a stranger who you may begin to build with, there are probably lots of fears that come up. Regardless, you want to be careful not to view this new person through the same lens you viewed others who have hurt you. It takes courage to be intentional and say, "I refuse to let my past hurts impact my future relationships." It takes work and effort, but it takes courage to trust and open yourself up. When you feel the anxiety or fear of growing deeper in a relationship with a new person, notice it and give yourself grace. You can take baby steps into learning and trusting this new person, but make sure that your fears of being hurt are not impacting the way you show up. When you do that, it takes away the chance for this new person to get to know the real you.

When shifting an acquaintance into a new position in your life such as a trusted source or friend, it can be nerve wracking. Many times, you may have heard things about them through other people or even had your own predispositions or judgements about them prior to getting to know them more intimately. It takes courage to say that, despite any negativity you may have heard from others, your desire is to build with them to get to know them.

I know some people may tell you that it's not wise to build with someone who others have spoken negatively about, but I would beg to differ. I personally think that every person deserves a chance to be known without judgment. This also means that you may have to choose to deflect or pause negative conversations about that person from others given that you want to protect your view of them before getting to know them for yourself.

Put yourself in their shoes. What if everyone had nothing but negative things to say about them? What if those things actually weren't true and were rumors? Imagine if you would have approached your relationship with them based off what others had to say. I'm a fan of giving others a chance, not just because rumors may not be true, but also because people have the right and ability to change and evolve.

For example, there may be people who knew me in high school who would have described me as mean or rude. However, I've evolved into a completely different human since then and their opinions of me are no longer valid because they don't have perspective on the person I am today. There are countless other reasons why you cannot just believe whatever you hear others say about people, but it's your job to make the courageous decision to love others beyond what you've heard about them.

Getting to know a complete stranger is a risk, but even your closest friends were once strangers. Sometimes you have to go through the awkward discomfort of being strangers and getting to the point where a relationship is fruitful and healthy. You have to make risky decisions like that if you want to have healthy friendships and relationships in the Promised Land. It may be hard to trust others, but it's a journey. You do not have to tell everyone every little detail about your life from the beginning. You can take your time getting to know a person and learn to build trust over time.

It's God's desire for you to have healthy friendships and people you can count on. It takes courage to let people in and I encourage you to be open to it!

## Deciding to take it slow in a relationship

Proverbs 12:26 NKJV tells us, "The righteous should choose his friends carefully, For the way of the wicked leads them astray." The Bible is clear that we should be careful in our approach to choosing friends and relationships. While it may be exciting to meet someone new and dive right in, there's wisdom in choosing relationships carefully.

Sometimes our trauma from the past causes us to push everyone away for fear that they hurt us. In turn, when we find a new person, we may cling to them and hold them tight. Maybe you've had poor romantic relationships in the past so when you find a new potential partner who you start to click with, you move extremely fast because it feels safe. Or maybe you've dealt with a ton of betrayal with friendships and you find a new friend who seems trustworthy, and everything just clicks. This friend feels like a breath of fresh air so now they become your go-to person for almost everything and you pull them super close because it feels safe.

While both scenarios may happen and cause no harm, sometimes pulling someone so close to you too quickly can be harmful. You may not pay attention to red flags, or you may become too dependent on the relationship very quickly. In either situation, you're robbing yourself of the chance to ease into a relationship with wisdom and caution.

I've learned that some people, not all people, struggle with this. They're often calling someone "best friend" within just a few short weeks or months of knowing them. Or they're jumping into romantic relationships quickly that advance quickly, too.

I believe that it's healthy and courageous to take things slow and with ease. Relationships are key in the Promised Land, and it's important to do yourself justice by choosing carefully as you build.

## Cutting ties with a friend

On the journey to your Promised Land, you'll have to evaluate your friendships and relationships. Everybody cannot go with you into the Promised Land. If we are honest with ourselves, we can say that not every relationship we've ever had has been chosen carefully and with wisdom. This means that as you go into the Promised Land, you may have to let some of those relationships go.

Have you ever wondered what the children of Israel were doing in the wilderness for forty years? Some of the people that were on their way into the Promised Land did not believe God though He fully proved Himself to them time and time again. So, in turn, God denied a part of the group entry into the Promised Land and the Israelites had to wait to enter until that group was no longer with them.

Joshua 5:6 NIV reads:

> "The Israelites had moved about in the wilderness forty years until all the men who were of military age when they left Egypt had died, since they had not obeyed the Lord. For the Lord had sworn to them that they would not see the land he had solemnly promised their ancestors to give us, a land flowing with milk and honey."

This verse really highlights something major. Some people were denied entry into the Promised Land simply because God said they could not enter.

What does that mean for you? Not everyone can go where you're headed. There may be relationships that you're holding onto that are not conducive to where God is taking you. It's okay, but sometimes you may have to cut ties with certain people and other times you may have to shift your perspective on where they belong in your circle. Not everyone can be a part of your inner circle. Not everybody can handle being in a friendship or relationship with you. It's your job to take inventory of who stays and who goes. Sometimes all you have to do is ask God to reveal who needs to be removed and He will make a way for the transition to happen.

Proverbs 13:20 NLT states, "Walk with the wise and become wise; associate with fools and get in trouble." Build your relationship with people who can support you with wisdom in the Promised Land. If the relationship doesn't align with your promise, chances are it won't last in the Promised Land. Making the courageous decision to end a relationship with a friend or partner is one that has a great impact on your life.

There is so much power in your decisions. I believe that there are some decisions you make in obedience to God that accelerate your forward movement in alignment with God's plan for your life. I call these Courageous Destiny Decisions. My decision to break up with my boyfriend after college was a decision like this and so was my decision to quit my six-figure corporate job. The chart below is a depiction of what I believe happens when you make a Courageous Destiny Decision.

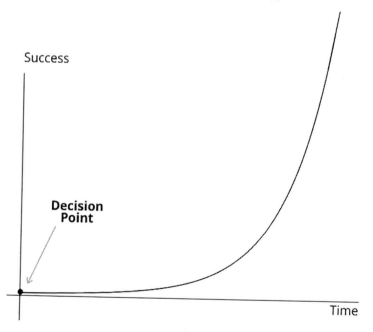

Your decisions can put you in position to accelerate what God is already doing in your life. We will dig more into this Courageous Destiny Decision chart later, but here's what I want to point out now: your decisions have the ability to take your success off the charts if you let it. That's the power of being in alignment with God, hearing His voice, and obeying when you hear what He says.

I find that it's helpful to have a plan of action when you're making decisions. I try to come up with a plan for making tough decisions when I'm sober-minded and not impacted by anything else. I've gone out of my way to even fast at times, read my Bible more, or pray more frequently in times where I really need to make a hard decision. Your plan to help you make decisions may look different from mine, but I encourage you to go put one together to help you make decisions that could shift your life.

---

**Take some time to reflect on this chapter and answer the following questions to help you shift your life in preparation for your promise.**

1. What's your Decision-Making Plan to help you make hard decisions?

2. Are there any courageous decisions you need to make?

3. Create a list of your relationships. Determine which ones are healthy and could enter your Promised Land.

4. Ask God which relationships you need to let go of to enter the next level of your Promised Land.

# 6 *Bold & Courageous Faith*

When God makes a promise, it's something we can trust. Trust in God is the foundation of our faith. We serve the one true and living God who gives us the power to speak to a mountain and tell it to move. But when we are faced with a mountain, we have options on how we respond to it. Sometimes we become accustomed to being intimidated by mountains that we become timid when we face them. The reality is that we have the power to *speak* to a mountain and it must obey.

> "Truly I tell you, if anyone says to this mountain, 'Go, throw yourself into the sea,' and does not doubt in their heart but believes that what they say will happen, it will be done for them" (Mark 11:23 NIV).

Wow. That's powerful. Let that sink in. You, my friend, have the ability to speak to a mountain and it will be moved.

Don't let the presence of a mountain make you lose sight of God's promise. The mountain may be in your way causing you to feel like God's promise is far out of sight, but in reality God may have allowed that mountain to be in your way just so that He can continue to build your faith. God's desire is for you to walk in the authority He has given you. You have the authority in God to speak to a mountain and carry on. But here's the catch: you have to believe that the mountain will be moved when you speak.

Think about it. Speaking to a physical mountain with the expectation for it to move sounds absurd. It would likely make the average person feel a bit uncomfortable. If you add a crowd into the mix, then it may make it a little more uncomfortable. But courage requires discomfort. You have to get out of your comfort zone if you want to see the miraculous happen in your life. You have to build up your strength to say that despite what you see, you're going to stand on God's promises and trust what He said.

Bold and courageous decisions are made with faith. I've always loved the concept of faith. Faith in God is rooted in pure, unadulterated belief and trust in God. It requires that you remove logic out of the picture so that you can believe the unbelievable.

Faith really only comes up when in tough situations or situations where you *need* God to really move on your behalf. But I believe that our faith is what activates God's movement. We cannot just sit back and expect to float into the Promised Land without taking any actions.

Once we become decided about something, we must move. Decision alone is not enough. Making a decision happens in your mind, but it takes faith to take action.

Having faith does not mean that you are not afraid. It just means that despite fear, you will make the decision to move forward. In the Bible, Hebrews 11:1 NKJV defines faith as: "Now faith is the substance of things hoped for, the evidence of things not seen." For the longest as a kid I never really understood this verse. However, I've grown to know that this really just means that faith is the thing that anchors our belief. It's the thing that we place our hope in and it explains the unexplainable.

The entire chapter of Hebrews 11 is a great passage to understand the purpose of faith and the role it plays in your journey as a Christian. Hebrews 11:3 NIV states, "By faith we understand that the universe was formed at God's command, so that what is seen was not made out of what was visible." This means that even God had faith to speak the world into existence. He had to believe that when He spoke something would shift. Faith had the ability to take something that was not visible and turn it into something tangible — a tangible universe. I want you to pause and think about the magnitude of the universe and how it was brought into existence by way of faith.

Imagine what your faith can do on your journey to and through the Promised Land. And let's take it a step further. Hebrews 11:6 NIV states, "And without faith it is impossible to please God, because anyone who comes to him must believe that he exists and that he rewards those who earnestly seek him." We must understand that our role is never to figure out God's plan, but rather, we should trust His plan and have faith that He will do exactly what He said He would do.

When it comes to our purpose and our Promised Land, we are not to just stand still and watch God move. We have an active role to play in our own destiny. It's spiritually unwise and immature to sit back and say, "I know God is going to do it" with reference to your future and destiny and not to expect to play a significant role in all of it. Yes, miracles are happening and will happen, but there is such a thing as aligning yourself so that you can experience the miraculous.

You may have heard this time and time again, but I want you to slow down and read this next sentence. James 2:26 NIV states, "As the body without the spirit is dead, so faith without deeds is dead." You may have heard the phrase "faith without works is dead". Imagine faith being a lifeless body without a spirit. That's exactly what faith is without action behind it… it's a lifeless body with no spirit. The thing that invigorates the body of faith is your action.

Yes, God will move, but you, my friend, will have to move, too. Even when it was time for me to quit my job, though I had to make the decision to quit, I had to take action on it. As soon as I took action toward what I believed, I was able to ignite my faith and show up with expectation that God would do what He said He would do.

One of my favorite verses in the Bible is Ephesians 3:20 NKJV which states: "Now to Him who is able to do exceedingly abundantly above all that we ask or think, according to the power that works in us,". I love it because not only does it state that God will do above and beyond what we can fathom, but we have a role in all of it. We have to ask and imagine. We also have to tap into the power that works in us. Romans 8:11 shares, "The Spirit of God, who raised Jesus from the dead, lives in you. And just as God raised Christ Jesus from the dead, he will give life to your mortal bodies by this same Spirit living within you."

When you realize the same power that raised Jesus from the dead is alive in you, you will begin to shift your actions accordingly. Sometimes your decisions won't make sense but you have to trust your history with God and trust that He will be faithful to do just what He said.

Let's take it back to Joshua and the children of Israel. God was giving them the land they swore to his forefathers. God promised Abraham and Sarah a child and promised that this child would be the start to Abraham being a father of many generations. The children of Israel were descendants of Abraham, and for a very long time Abraham and his wife Sarah were without children because Sarah could not conceive a child.

Let's look at Hebrews 11:11 BSB which states, "By faith Sarah, even though she was barren and beyond the proper age, was enabled to conceive a child, because she considered Him faithful who had promised." Not only was Sarah able to conceive, but she birthed a son who was the fulfillment of the promise that God had for her in her lifetime.

It was Sarah's faith that made it possible for her to give birth to a child. It was Sarah's faith that allowed room for God's promise to fully actualize. You, too, have to play a role in God's promise for your life. You have to believe that God will be faithful to do exactly what He said He would do. Plus, let's not forget that God cares, so He wants to give you the desires of your heart.

You will have to make the conscious effort to move past your trauma and past hurt to still choose to believe. Maybe, like Sarah, you're believing God for a child that He promised you. Maybe you've experienced miscarriage after miscarriage and you're struggling to believe that what God said is true. Maybe you even laughed at God like Sarah did when He told Abraham she was going to give birth in her old age.

Let's talk about why Sarah could have laughed. I've learned from my lovely inner healing counselor that laughing is a coping or soothing mechanism to avoid the reality of your pain. We will never know exactly why Sarah laughed, but I can imagine it was because she was coping with her pain. She had been believing in God for decades to have a child and now God was going to give her the promise in her old age. I believe Sarah had been let down time and time again while waiting on the promise. She even went about things her own way and had her husband, Abraham, sleep with their servant, Hagar, in an attempt to bring forth the child God promised. When that didn't work out, I believe she was let down. So, I believe Sarah may have laughed to keep from crying from the pain of her promise not yet being realized.

I want to stop and encourage you to never stop believing God for what He promised. No matter what you've been through, and no matter how many times you feel like you've been let down, God's promise still stands.

When it was time for me to quit my job in corporate America, I kept asking so many people a question they couldn't answer: "What's the difference between having crazy faith versus walking in wisdom?"

I now know that the difference is that crazy faith is based on you being led by God to do what He calls you to do. So, if you heard Him say it or if you felt it in your heart to do it, it's yours for the taking.

Crazy faith requires you trust God even when it doesn't make sense. I believe that crazy faith allows you to have a space in your life where miracles happen. I also believe that God confirms His promise multiple times to reassure you that He said what He said. For you, this may look like the dots being connected. This may look like receiving a prophetic word like I did. This may look like God speaking to you through the word of God. It may look like listening to a sermon that tells you that you're right on track. Regardless, God always delivers on His promise so it's your job to align and believe that He will be faithful to do what He said He would do.

I've made lots of scary decisions that have turned into bold and courageous decisions. I did them each with faith, trusting that God would deliver every time. When I quit my job in corporate America, the $15,000 I'd asked for was deposited into my bank the day after my last day at work. I remember the feeling of knowing that God had done exactly what He said he would do, and I was personally mind blown. It was that experience that built my faith to believe God for more in the future.

I often say that it's my history with God that allows me to believe that God can do a hard thing. One of my first experiences with faith was as a student in high school. I kept saying and believing that I would get a full-ride scholarship to pay for all my tuition and room and board. So, what did I do? I applied for as many scholarships as possible during my lunch break and I made sure to apply for all the available scholarship programs at the schools I was attending. Though there was no scholarship in sight, I kept telling my family and friends that I was going to get a full ride. I applied to a local scholarship and ended up receiving a full-tuition scholarship for my freshman year, but it did not cover all four years. I was excited about it, but I knew that this wasn't what God had promised me.

So, the date arrived when I had to declare what school I was attending and the best offer I got was to attend the University of Illinois at Urbana-Champaign's business program. I was really excited about it, but I'd only gotten one year of school covered financially though my heart was set on getting all four years paid for. I trusted that God was moving so I believed that regardless of what happened I would trust that God would make sure that all four years of my college was covered. So, I cheerfully accepted the scholarship to attend the University of Illinois Urbana-Champaign, and I paid for the move-in registration fee.

About a few weeks after I'd decided to go to my local state school, I received a phone call from the head of financial aid at Washington University in St. Louis. He asked why I had not decided to attend the school and I told him it was because my parents did not have the finances to cover the nearly $60,000 per year tuition. After listening to me, he told me to take a look online to check out my new financial aid package they had offered me, and I was in shock. I cried when I saw what I was offered. I received a full-tuition scholarship including room and board. It was exactly what God had promised me as a senior in high school and I gladly accepted and attended college at Washington University in St. Louis.

That experience with God as a young adult really started to build my faith and show me that God could do the impossible. He came later than I thought, but it was literally right on time. That one phone call had made it possible for me to attend college and only have to focus on my coursework and living expenses beyond the basics. I quickly learned that God is a God who delivers on His promises.

When it comes to your journey with faith, I encourage you to remember what God has done for you in the past. Remember the moments where you were faced with the impossible, yet God made a way out of no way. Remember the moments when God showed up late, but right on time. Remember that God has never let you down in the past, and it won't start anytime soon.

There was one point on my faith journey when I literally uttered the words: "I know God has never failed me, but if it ever felt like it, this is what it feels like." So, I want to talk to you about what happens when the faith that you have doesn't work out the way you thought. What do you do when you feel like God failed you and you feel like your faith did not do what it was supposed to?

In 2019, I had been building my businesses successfully for three years. Epic Fab Girl had started getting traction and growing an audience and membership of people who I was able to help build their businesses. My marketing company, Candace Junée Marketing, had been helping clients grow their businesses, and I was getting coaching clients and speaking engagements that were bringing in consistent income. That September, I had scheduled Epic Fab Girl's Go-Getter Conference in Chicago and knew that God told me to host it. I believed that God was going to do something miraculous through it. Epic Fab Girl was not making substantial income to be able to put on an expensive conference, so I made the decision to invest my money from my marketing business to put on this conference. I made the decision to invest my personal money into the business and forego paying my mortgage and car note because I believed that I would be able to generate money after the conference to pay for it.

The 2019 conference came, and God moved mightily, but I walked away with $11,000 in debt and no idea how to pay it. After the conference, I went back to my condo in Chicago to find out that my internet was off because I was behind on payments. So, I was broke, without internet, and starting to spiral into the worst depression I'd ever experienced. One of my closest friends already had a trip planned for us to Mexico that October so I left the country knowing that my life was in shambles back at home.

At that point, everything I had previously tried in business to gain income was no longer working. It was like I was stuck in business and no matter what I did I was not able to generate enough income. When I got back to Chicago, I fell behind on my mortgage and my car got repossessed. I sat there questioning every decision I'd made in faith. I was previously so confident that God had told me to host the conference, but here I was looking at the facts of my situation and it felt like I had failed God and it felt like He had failed me. I felt like I must have heard God wrong. It felt like I must have not heard Him correctly, and for some reason, He thought it was okay to let me down. During all of that, God reassured me that I would not lose my home.

September through December 2019 were some of the darkest moments I'd ever experienced in life. During that season, I had to make the decision to pray when I didn't feel like it. I had to trust God when I didn't feel like it. I had to push forward even though I thought that God had forgotten about me. On December 26, 2019, I was served foreclosure papers on my home. As if my situation could not get any worse, I felt completely trapped by pursuing the Promised Land that God had given me.

I was so confused because for so long I knew God had promised me great success in business, but here I was…struggling to pay my mortgage, my car note, my internet, and so much more. Even though I was disappointed in where I was, and my faith wavered, I never completely lost faith in the fact that God would deliver me and that I had made the right decision to quit my job in corporate America.

During that time, so many people kept telling me that they thought I should just go get a job in corporate America just for the time being to pay for my expenses. It made logical sense to do since I had two degrees, but I personally knew God did not tell me to do that. Every time I prayed about it; God would not give me peace about applying for a job.

God's job for me in that season was to trust His plan A instead of trying to depend on an alternate plan B or C. It was a long and hard season, but it required for me to continue to press into God, pray, read my Word, and remind God of what He had promised me. I was depressed, but I didn't lose my faith.

I was at such a low place that I hadn't even told my family that my home was at serious risk of foreclosure. My parents had already stepped up a few times and took on the financial strain to help me pay my mortgage, but this time they could not help. I had no energy to work with clients. I had no energy to keep trying. I just kept posting on Instagram from my bed finding strength to encourage others to trust God and giving them encouraging words when I was struggling to stay encouraged myself.

One day I was laying in bed feeling completely defeated, and my father called me. I didn't want to pick up, but I did. I didn't want to hear, "I told you so," or any other negativity I'd learned to expect from him. I could barely speak because I was so worn out and he heard it in my voice. He asked me what was wrong, and I still couldn't formulate much of a sentence. He said, "Okay, Candace, let's pray." I proceeded to tell my dad the words, "No, I don't want to pray."

To my surprise, my dad perked up and started going in on me in the best way possible. Instead of what he had traditionally done in the past, he began to speak life into me. He said, "What do you mean you don't want to pray? Do you know the God we serve?" My dad went on for about ten minutes encouraging me and praying for me and over my life. Though my dad had been someone who'd I be able to call in the past for a quick prayer, I'd never seen him pour into me in this way. It was exactly what I needed at the moment to keep the faith. Not only that, but it also helped me to shift my view of him and have better interactions with him as an adult.

My relationship with my father had been rocky over the years and was steadily improving, but that conversation shifted my perspective. I heard exactly what I needed to hear to feel his love and encouragement. Even if God had to bring me to my lowest just so that my father could speak life into me and I could restore my view of him, that was all I needed.

I was so encouraged and uplifted. Though my situation didn't turn around immediately, I knew that God was up to something miraculous in nature.

By February 2020, I had to show up in court regarding the foreclosure. I walked into the courtroom and approached the judge's stand. To my surprise, the judge let me walk out that day and gave me a ton of grace. She told me to give it time and she would reach back out if we needed a future court date. When I left the room, I literally wanted to shout and jump with joy because I was beginning to see that God was working something out that I could not understand.

By March of 2020, the COVID-19 Pandemic forced fore-closures to be halted. It was literally a move of God on my behalf. Not only did it delay the process with my foreclosure, but by July of 2021 I would be able to sell my property for more than I purchased it for, and I did not have to pay the bank a dime. I was so blessed because I knew that typically people have to sell their homes in a short sale, when in my situation, God came through and did something so miracu-lous that it was unbelievable.

I have learned that even when you feel like God has failed you, it just means that God is not finished yet. Period. Don't lose faith in your process. Trust and believe that whatever God said He would do, He will do.

In 2020 I went from having $0 in the bank to building a six-figure business, and that was nothing but the grace of God. Through a series of miraculous events and me walking in what God told me to do, I was able to put my business knowledge to work and build a successful business. That's exactly why I will always give God glory because I know that none of the success I have or will ever attain will be because of me, it will literally be nothing but God.

Now I want to talk to you about something that may get in the way of your faith: safety disguised as discernment. Sometimes we think we're walking in "wisdom" by playing it safe, when in reality we're delaying our own entry into the Promised Land. Of course, we want to be wise about our decisions, but that doesn't mean that you shouldn't take risks. There's no wisdom in playing it safe when it comes to faith.

Don't cover up your fear and call it discernment saying that you want to be wise with your decisions. Only you know if you're really just playing scared or if you're moving in the direction God called you to. Either way, there's a fine line between the two. Make sure your decisions are really getting you closer to the version of your future that God promised and isn't just keeping you stagnant.

As a part of your journey to living in everything God has for you, your prayer life is essential. You have to be willing to pray bold prayers. Just like Peter was able to communicate with Jesus and ask a bold request to walk on water, you, too, must position yourself to make bold requests of God. Hebrews 4:16 NKJV states, "Let us therefore come boldly to the throne of grace, that we may obtain mercy and find grace to help in time of need." Our role as Christians is to approach God boldly with our prayers in our moments of need. Sometimes we may have to pray prayers that don't make sense logically. Sometimes we have to believe the unexpected and pray to God that He will see it through. That's the type of faith and prayers that gives us the power to walk on water.

Prayer is nothing more than conversation and communication with God. Your Promised Land requires communication with God for direction, insight, and courage. It was God's conversation with Joshua that gave him the courage to move forward in the face of fear.

There will be times when God speaks to you loud and clear, and there will be times when you feel like you can't hear God at all. Let your conversations with God lead you into your next steps. If you ever feel like you cannot hear clearly from God, I encourage you to fast and eliminate noise in your life so that you can hear from God more clearly. However, I do believe that there are times when God is intentionally quiet. I believe those are the moments when God is building your faith and simply wants you to trust Him. Your job is not to know the full plan, rather, your job is to follow God's plan one step at a time, even if it feels like you don't know where you're going.

Conversations with God are game-changing. I was bold enough to pray to God and ask for a date to leave my corporate job and God gave me a date. I was bold enough to ask for $15,000 to move forward with the vision God had for me as a full-time entrepreneur. I was bold enough to ask for overflow when there was nothing but desolation all around me. Bold and courageous prayers are the ones that you pray even when your situation and circumstances don't make sense.

You have to be willing to lay it all on the line and pray to God with the expectation that He will answer. You have to pray bold prayers like Sarah and trust that God will be faithful to fulfill His promise.

But what happens when it feels like faith doesn't work? What happens when you pray and believe God for a miracle, and it doesn't happen? What happens when you stand on faith and consistently believe God, but the outcome doesn't happen as you planned? What happens when you obey God, but your life still ends up in shambles? I know you may have been through many moments in life where your prayers were not answered. You know what I mean. The moments in life where you believed for a miracle, but you still felt like you were in a pit. The moments that gnawed away at your faith because you felt like God failed you. What do you do then?

Whenever you feel like your faith is failing because God did not respond the way you desired or expected, it's time for you to shift your perspective. You have to understand that God has an eternal viewpoint of your life. You have to trust that maybe God's not done yet. Maybe the story isn't over yet. Maybe God is using (or allowed) the situation to build your faith to another level.

What do you do to build your faith when you feel like all hope is gone? My answer is simple and biblical. Build your faith by reading the Word of God. Romans 10:17 NKJV says, "So then faith comes by hearing, and hearing by the word of God." Immerse yourself in the Word of God and watch your perspective be transformed. Of course, you may not feel like reading the Bible when you're feeling down or depressed. I've been there. But give it time and allow yourself the space to sit with and read the Bible or even listen to it on audio.

I personally believe that miracle moments are simultaneously some of the messiest moments of life. We have to be okay with God allowing for our lives to get messy before He brings about miracles. When your life and situation are a mess, there's always going to be the temptation to abandon God and give up on believing Him. That's what the enemy wants. He wants you to stop believing what God said.

When I was raped in 2021, I felt that situation was built to break me. It was a scheme designed by the enemy to coerce me into walking away from God and abandoning my calling. I desperately wanted to quit walking in purpose because I felt like my decision to follow God made me a constant open target for the enemy. I felt like the personal and spiritual attacks were only coming because of my decision to obey and follow God.

I'm giving myself the freedom to be raw and open with you because you're reading my book. I'm considering you a judgment-free zone, so... can I be real with you? Something inside me wanted to walk away from God completely. I felt so hurt and broken that God would allow something so horrific to happen. For the longest, I couldn't find it in me to have faith. I was depleted. I completely lost hope.

Somewhere along the journey I realized that this was the enemy's plan all along. To try to make me stop believing God and to try to make me walk in less authority. It took some time, but when I realized that, I made the conscious effort to walk in my authority and fight from a place of faith because God was with me.

God used that situation to help me to see another level of authority. If I can make a decision to pick up the pieces in my life and move forward with faith, so can you. Be encouraged to know that it's possible for you.

Sometimes God will use strange situations to bring about miracles in your life. Sometimes God will bring about miracles when your life and everything around you is a mess. Your job is to believe God and put your faith in Him, even when it's difficult.

God never changes. He's a healer, restorer, friend, and provider. He's so much more than that, but He's never going to allow you to walk through a mess He can't turn into a miracle.

I believe your Promised Land requires you to not only have faith in God but faith in yourself and your abilities. We'll talk much more about that in chapter eight, but for now we're going to focus on dealing with what you may have to sacrifice on the journey to the Promised Land.

# 7 Bold & Courageous Sacrifices

Your journey into the Promised Land requires many sacrifices. One of the main things you will have to sacrifice is your comfort. Your journey to the Promised Land will make you uncomfortable, but it will stretch you in the best way possible.

I have personally had to sacrifice so much to get to where I am now. In the last chapter, you saw how I sacrificed paying my mortgage and car note to walk in purpose. While I do not recommend financial irresponsibility, I do, however, fully recommend trusting God and doing what He tells you to do. I'm not telling you to go out and skip out on paying your bills, rather, I'm telling you that when you align with God, you will be led to do what He tells you to do.

By the end of the first quarter of 2020, I had landed a new marketing client and my income increased to multiple four figure months. I was able to breathe a little easier. I was able to start paying down debts that I owed, but I was not truly able to fully get ahead. However, I knew that 2020 was a year that God wanted me to shift into the best year I'd ever experienced. God showed me that He was getting ready to give me beauty for ashes.

I spent the beginning of 2020 consistently fasting and praying to hear God's voice. I wanted to make sure that I heard God clearly and that I clung tightly to Him. God led me to host a virtual Go-Getter Conference experience early in the year. The previous year we had hosted it in August, but God made it clear that it should be in April. I began reaching out to speakers in February and planned every detail out. I had no idea the world would experience a pandemic, but God positioned me to host the virtual conference in the middle of lockdown. I followed God's instructions precisely regarding the free virtual event and wasn't really focused much on the financial impact that it would make. As I was preparing for the event, God asked me how I was going to monetize, and I quickly came up with a strategy to test. With God's guidance, that conference generated the first five-figure month I'd ever experienced in business, and it was multiple five-figures. I was completely mind-blown.

God began to turn my world around and I promised that He would get the glory out of all of it. I had made many sacrifices leading up to this point, and I knew that God was calling me to another level.

I believe that every level you're going to ascend to requires another level of sacrifice. Our obedience to God requires that we sacrifice something, and, for me, the sacrifice came in many different forms. I had to sacrifice the comfort of my six-figure corporate job. I had to sacrifice paying for my bills in lieu of my purpose. I had to sacrifice the ability to know the full plan. I had to sacrifice relationships that were not adding value to my life though I loved the people dearly. But now it was time for another level of sacrifice to get to my next level.

I want to pause for a moment to take us back to the story of Joshua and the children of Israel. Before Joshua ever became a leader of the children of Israel, God made a promise to Abraham about his descendants. We'll take a closer look at this story in Genesis.

> "But Abram said, 'Sovereign Lord, what can you give me since I remain childless and the one who will inherit my estate is Eliezer of Damascus?' And Abram said, 'You have given me no children; so a servant in my household will be my heir.' Then the word of the Lord came to him: 'This man will not be your heir, but a son who is your own flesh and blood will be your heir.' He took him outside and said, 'Look up at the sky and count the stars — if indeed you can count them.' Then he said to him, 'So shall your offspring be'" (Genesis 15:2-4 NIV).

> "Then the Lord said to him, 'Know for certain that for four hundred years your descendants will be strangers in a country not their own and that they will be enslaved and mistreated there. But I will punish the nation they serve as slaves, and afterward they will come out with great possessions. You, however, will go to your ancestors in peace and be buried at a good old

age. In the fourth generation your descendants will come back here, for the sin of the Amorites has not yet reached its full measure'" (Genesis 15:13-16 NIV).

"On that day the Lord made a covenant with Abram and said, 'To your descendants I give this land, from the Wadi of Egypt to the great river, the Euphrates — the land of the Kenites, Kenizzites, Kadmonites, Hittites, Perizzites, Rephaites, Amorites, Canaanites, Girgashites and Jebusites'" (Genesis 15:18 NIV).

God made a significant promise to Abraham when he was without children. His wife had been unable to conceive, and God showed up with a promise that his descendants would compare in number to the stars. What an amazing promise, but can you imagine how Abraham felt when God showed him that and the promise was nowhere in sight?

If you know anything about the story of Abraham and Sarah, you know they both grew tired of waiting on the fulfillment of the promise. So, Sarah came up with a plot to have Abraham sleep with their servant Hagar and she became pregnant so that Abraham could have a son. Of course, that was not God's original plan and down the line God eventually came to Abraham and confirmed that He would deliver on His original promise.

Genesis 18:10 states that God confirmed to Abraham that, "I will return to you about this time next year, and your wife, Sarah, will have a son!" Genesis 21:1-2 NLT explains, "The Lord kept his word and did for Sarah exactly what he had promised. She became pregnant, and she gave birth to a son for Abraham in his old age. This happened at just the time God had said it would."

Abraham waited years to have the fulfillment of this promise that God had for he and his wife. So, imagine how ecstatic Abraham was knowing that God would do exactly what He said He would by providing him a son and giving him numerous descendants.

In Genesis 22, we learn that God makes a seemingly ridiculous request of Abraham.

> "Some time later God tested Abraham. He said to him, 'Abraham!'. 'Here I am,' he replied. Then God said, 'Take your son, your only son, whom you love — Isaac — and go to the region of Moriah. Sacrifice him there as a burnt offering on a mountain I will show you'" (Genesis 22:1-2 NIV).

Wildly enough, Abraham complied. Watch what happens next:

> "When they reached the place God had told him about, Abraham built an altar there and arranged the wood on it. He bound his son Isaac and laid him on the altar, on top of the wood. Then he reached out his hand and took the knife to slay his son.
>
> But the angel of the Lord called out to him from heaven, 'Abraham! Abraham!'. 'Here I am,' he replied. 'Do not lay a hand on the boy,' he said. 'Do not do anything to him. Now I know that you fear God, because you have not withheld from me your son, your only son.'

> Abraham looked up and there in a thicket he saw a ram caught by its horns. He went over and took the ram and sacrificed it as a burnt offering instead of his son. So Abraham called that place The Lord Will Provide. And to this day it is said, 'On the mountain of the Lord it will be provided.'" (Genesis 22:9-14 NIV)

I personally believe that Abraham's story is a beautiful display of just how much God desires for us to trust Him. God's desire for us is to want a right relationship with Him more than we want the promise. Yes, the Promised Land is a beautiful place to exist and the promises within it are phenomenal to experience, but we must never forget that God is the ultimate reward.

Sacrifice comes from a place of choosing God's plan over our own. It's about you standing up and saying that your trust in God is what's most important despite your own logic. God is the promise keeper but also the promise giver. God will always make good on His promises, so it's your job to comply and obey no matter what.

Imagine what Abraham must have been feeling before placing his son on the altar of sacrifice. He may have been feeling deep pain wondering "Why Me" or "Why God". He may have been thinking why would God take me through all this waiting just to face even more pain and watch me kill my son and have to live with that forever? He may have thought that this is such a cruel request. I can imagine that Abraham was torn to pieces, but you can tell that Abraham has journeyed with God long enough to know that God is sovereign, and He has all the plans figured out.

By this point, Abraham had made several mistakes over the years by disobeying God. Now God testing Abraham's trust in God by telling him to sacrifice his only son. God had to make sure that He could trust Abraham with the promise.

Now, if you ask me anything about sacrifice, I'll tell you it is painful. Before I quit my job in corporate America, I had to start cutting back my expenses. That meant that I no longer had it in my budget to get my nails and hair done as consistently. I was no longer able to spend as much money on hobbies and extracurriculars. I had to focus and say no to things I actually wanted to say yes to. Even after I quit, my life shifted drastically. Though I never really wanted for anything, I had to sacrifice a lot. For a very long time, I did not purchase any new clothes, shoes, or anything that was not an absolute necessity. It was really hard because fashion was something I loved, and I sacrificed looking the way I wanted to.

There were other times I had to sacrifice what I was eating. I had to shop light at the grocery store and make my meals stretch throughout the week. There were times when I didn't have enough money to even buy groceries and then the next thing you know God provided for me by allowing someone to take me to get groceries for free. I have learned that sacrifices are real, they can be painful, but God will always be a provider. His provision may not always look the way you expect, but He will always provide. After a long journey of financial sacrifices and sacrifices to my lifestyle, I started to see a shift.

After having my first successful five-figure launch and generating consistent income in my businesses, God was calling me to step out even further in faith. By May of 2020, I was still in a position where I was getting caught up on bills, but I wanted to be intentional about my growth in business. I felt God calling me to find a coach to help me along the journey, and He made it clear that it should be someone who was faith based. I did some research and waited a while to make a decision, but when I found a coach that I thought would be great for me, I was not in a financial position to invest the full amount of the program. The investment for the program was $7,500, but I only had the initial $2,500 investment.

At first, I was nervous to say yes to the sacrifice because I wasn't sure if I'd be able to make the remaining payments. I prayed about it some more, and I was certain that God was up to something, so I said yes to the program not knowing how I'd be able to pay for everything else.

When I made that financial sacrifice, I made the decision to take myself, my business, and my expertise seriously. I began getting way more consistent with social media and implemented the strategies that my coach gave me. In under a month, I was able to generate $31,000 in sales and again, I was mind-blown. But more than anything, it gave me the confidence to know that what I had to offer really worked for people. When I taught my clients their strategies to make money in their businesses, it worked for them too, and I became a little more confident and convinced of my power even though I'd been teaching these same strategies for years.

Sometimes you may have to make a sacrifice that doesn't make sense. Sometimes you may have to risk it all for something that may pay off in the long run. If we use Abraham's story as an example, God will provide a ram in the bush in necessary situations. However, our focus should never be on God providing the way out, rather we should focus on honing in on really trusting God. That is the place where you can show up as the unapologetic expert. You're literally making a decision to say that regardless of how crazy you may look or how absurd your instructions from God may be, you trust God.

If we look at Abraham's example, we see that this sacrifice was a thing between him and God. In that story there were servants that helped Abraham get to the place where he would sacrifice his son. His servants were unaware of the plan between him and God so he left them behind in the distance. Some sacrifices are just kept between you and God. Some sacrifices are not meant for others to understand simply because those were not instructions given to them, those instructions were directly from God to you.

My best advice to you is to make your decision to take risks from a place of peace. Whether you're making a decision to sacrifice something major or you're uncertain about the outcome of something, I challenge you to lean into God and trust that He knows the final plan. If you don't have peace about a decision, don't make the decision. Wait until you get the peace and feel cleared to make the decision.

When you fully trust God and what He's telling you to do, then you can position yourself to have full confidence in yourself and your ability. Regardless of where you're at in your journey, it's time for you to bet on yourself regardless of what you have to sacrifice.

# 8 *Bold & Courageous Confidence*

Confidence within yourself helps others to trust you as a leader and an expert. The more confident you are, the more others can trust that you really, truly know what you're talking about. I've learned that confident, trustworthy leaders are not ones who aggressively assert their authority over others, rather they are those who speak from a place of confidence. They speak to others only to build them up and never to tear them down. Those are the leaders who thrive best in the Promised Land. Confidence and arrogance are not the same thing.

Owning your brilliance is what you should do as a confident leader. At the end of the day, you should not have to diminish your shine to make others feel comfortable. This does not mean that you lack humility and integrity. You can be humble, kind, AND confident. That does not equal arrogance. When I say "own your brilliance" that means to fully accept the amazing masterpiece you are and confidently move forward with that in mind. Confidence doesn't always come easy, though. Oftentimes we may wrestle with our traumas from the past, insecurities, anxieties and so much more on the journey to becoming truly confident. My best advice is to embrace the journey and don't rush your process.

Confidence is a decision you have to make daily. It's something you have to fight for. You must decide to show up confidently. You must decide to make decisions with confidence to enter and thrive in your Promised Land. Confidence comes from within, and it starts with a decision within. There are so many things in our world that can easily impact your confidence and ability to flourish in your Promised Land.

When it comes to making decisions, it can be easy to focus on everything external. We look at our environment, we look at our situation, and we weigh the cost. However, weighing the cost is not the problem. I've learned that so many people who struggle with taking radical leaps of faith struggle because they do not appropriately weigh the cost.

What do I mean by weighing the cost? I mean fully evaluating the situation to be able to make a decision. Luke 14:28 says, "For which of you, desiring to build a tower, does not first sit down and count the cost, whether he has enough to complete it?" In this situation, it refers to someone preparing to build a tower, who would have to count the cost prior to building. In the same way, I believe that we typically learn to weigh the cost before making decisions.

Let's take this tower analogy a little bit further. I've learned that many times people count the cost and choose not to build when the building was meant to be established. They abort the mission completely. I think it's because many people have become accustomed to weighing the cost, but they neglect to tap into their own power and the power of the Holy Spirit. So they count the cost based on what they know and what they can figure out on their own. But when we are talking about your Promised Land, we cannot solely depend on ourselves and our knowledge.

To make ground-shaking steps in the direction of your purpose, you need to count the cost and include God in the mix. God's power is manifested in the earth through the power of the Holy Spirit that lives in you. When you realize that you are creating, building, and walking with the Holy Spirit as a Christian, you show up differently. It's important to tap into the power of God and recognize who God is when you're making decisions. If God told you to do something and he has the ultimate power and plan, why not trust Him? Why not trust that He will have it all figured out.

Sure, your faith is going to be tested on your journey to and through the Promised Land, but God will be with you every step of the way. Every time you prepare to make a faith-filled decision, I want you to envision the Holy Spirit holding your hand and walking through it with you. Let me remind you who God is:

- Defender (Psalm 18:1)
- Protector (Psalm 18:2)
- Provider (Philippians 4:19)
- Strong Tower (Proverbs 18:10)

- Prince of Peace (Isaiah 9:6)
- Counselor (Isaiah 9:6)
- Mighty God (Isaiah 9:6)
- Everlasting Father (Isaiah 9:6)
- Wonderful (Isaiah 9:6)
- Healer (Luke 5:17-25)
- Deliverer (Psalm 40:17)
- Lover of Your Soul (John 3:16)
- Good Father (Matthew 7:11)
- Friend (John 15:15)
- Your Strength (2 Corinthians 12:9)

The list goes on and on, but let me remind you of a little more about who God is and what He does:

- He owns a cattle on a thousand hills. (Psalm 50:10)
- The earth is the His and the fullness thereof. (Psalm 24:1)
- The earth is His footstool. (Isaiah 66:1)
- He prepares a table for you in the presence of your enemies. (Psalm 23:5)
- He defeats your enemies. (Deuteronomy 28:7)
- The Lord will fight for you. (Exodus 14:14)

I want you to keep God and the power of the Holy Spirit in mind when you're making decisions. God is the one who created the plan for your life, and He knows how everything will work out. Yes, count the cost, but also trust that God is sovereign, and He will never let you down.

Let's jump back to the story of Joshua and the Children of Israel in the Bible. So, at this point, Joshua and nearly 40,000 people crossed the Jordan River. They camped out at a place called Gilgal and had Passover prior to entering the next city they were supposed to enter, Jericho. However, God still had not given Joshua any instructions on how to conquer the city of Jericho, which was the first city they needed to overtake in order to claim their territory in Canaan. As he neared Jericho, Joshua encountered an angel, and I'll let the Bible speak for itself here in Joshua 6:1-5 NIV:

> "Now the gates of Jericho were securely barred because of the Israelites. No one went out and no one came in. Then the Lord said to Joshua, 'See, I have delivered Jericho into your hands, along with its king and its fighting men.
>
> March around the city once with all the armed men. Do this for six days. Have seven priests carry trumpets of rams' horns in front of the ark. On the seventh day, march around the city seven times, with the priests blowing the trumpets.
>
> When you hear them sound a long blast on the trumpets, have the whole army give a loud shout; then the wall of the city will collapse and the army will go up, everyone straight in.'"

Joshua followed God's instructions and what happened next didn't make any sense at all, but God delivered on His promise. Check this out in Joshua 6:20 NIV:

"When the trumpets sounded, the army shouted, and at the sound of the trumpet, when the men gave a loud shout, the wall collapsed; so everyone charged straight in, and they took the city."

Joshua successfully led the children of Israel into the siege of the Promised Land. What I'm always amazed at is Joshua's radical and immediate obedience to God's instruction. God speaks and Joshua responds. God gave Joshua the play-by-play as it was happening, and not before. It makes sense, though, because God promised He would always be with Joshua. In that same way, God will always be with you. Joshua's story is powerful, and I believe it's a sign to what we can accomplish if we don't question our faith and God's sovereignty. It did not make logical sense to march around a city with the expectation for the walls guarding the city to fall. Let's also be clear that these walls were not your average drywall or brick wall. According to architect Ian Volner's article in *Time Magazine* entitled "Why Do People Build Walls? The Real Story of Jericho Offers a Surprising Answer," the walls of Jericho were "12 feet high and 6 feet wide at the base".

The walls of Jericho were massive, and it didn't make sense for marching and shouting to make them fall, but they did. And that, my friend, speaks to the brilliance, magnitude, and complete sovereignty of God.

God is sovereign and He will not let you down. David, King of Israel, the writer of Psalms even states years later in Psalm 37:25 NIV: "I have been young, and now am old;

yet have I not seen the righteous forsaken, nor his seed begging bread."

You have to harness God's love and His power to give you courage to make bold decisions. It may not be easy to do at times, but you have to learn to trust God more than you trust yourself and your environment.

Matthew 14:22-33 gives the account of Jesus walking on water. But did you know that Jesus was not the only man who was able to walk on water? Let's look at this story directly from Matthew 14:26-31 NIV:

> "Shortly before dawn Jesus went out to them, walking on the lake. When the disciples saw him walking on the lake, they were terrified. 'It's a ghost,' they said, and cried out in fear. But Jesus immediately said to them: 'Take courage! It is I. Don't be afraid.' 'Lord, if it's you,' Peter replied, 'tell me to come to you on the water.' 'Come,' he said. Then Peter got down out of the boat, walked on the water and came toward Jesus. But when he saw the wind, he was afraid and, beginning to sink, cried out, 'Lord, save me!' Immediately Jesus reached out his hand and caught him. 'You of little faith,' he said, 'why did you doubt?'"

Now, let's take a moment to focus on a part of the story that not many people focus on during sermons. Jesus's command to *all* of the disciples was to "take courage," however Peter was the only one to respond to Jesus asking Him to prove Himself to Peter so that he, too could walk on water. Peter was the only one with enough courage and faith in the moment to get out of the boat and onto the water. The other disciples were watching, but they missed out on the same opportunity because they did not even have the boldness to ask to walk on water, to get out of the boat, and to walk on water. This story could have ended very differently. God had the power to allow all the disciples to walk on water, but Peter was the only one bold enough to ask. Don't let your environment, including your friends and peers, hinder you from making bold requests of God.

Now let's focus on Peter's faith and his decisions. Peter decided to ask Jesus to prove himself. Peter decided to get out of the boat. Peter decided to walk on water. Once Peter got off of the boat, he began to defy the odds of science and any ounce of logic. Walking on water was completely illogical and seemingly impossible, but he saw Jesus do it and he knew that he could, too. The only problem was that Peter began to shift into a place of logic again by looking at the wind and waves, so he began to sink.

Remember, confidence is a decision you have to make. Peter had to make a series of decisions with faith and full confidence in God. Those decisions he made led him to getting out of the boat and onto the water, but then he began to panic. Peter decided to look at everything else but Jesus in that moment and panic and logic crept in.

I think so many of us end up like Peter. We make courageous moves of faith by obeying God and then we start focusing on the wrong things. We panic and find ourselves questioning our decisions to begin with. Very much like me when I quit my job in corporate America and found myself completely broke. I panicked. I was confused because I was confidently moving along before, but as soon as I began to pay attention to the facts of my environment, I began to sink.

We can learn so much from Peter's situation when he walked on water. All Peter needed to do was to trust himself and remain confident in the power that God had given him. Once Peter began to sink, Jesus' response was: "You of little faith. Why did you doubt?"

Why did Peter doubt? Peter's logic began to supersede his faith in God. His environment was beginning to cause him to choose doubt over faith. I believe we all end up in moments where we act on faith and begin to question what God said because of our environment. I challenge you to shift your mindset and stand in faith and confidence even when your environment doesn't look conducive to the miraculous.

God's desire is to do miraculous things in you and through you. God cannot achieve what He desires to do in your life without you making bold decisions to trust Him. Earlier in this book we learned how our fears may be impacting our decisions and confidence, and I want to revisit that to show you how to walk in confidence despite your fears.

One of the main things that God does to prepare you for the Promised Land is build your confidence. He builds your confidence in Him and your confidence in yourself. God's vision is to restore your self-image and self-view to His original intent and design. God wants you to see yourself the way that He sees you so that you can walk in full confidence in His plan for your life.

For me, becoming confident was difficult. It was something I had to fight for because the world had been tearing me down my entire life. I'd been defending myself and my existence for so long and had become so timid and afraid because of it. I was moving around by tiptoeing to avoid negative opinions of others and to avoid failing, but God had to restore my view of myself so that I could fulfill my purpose and the call He had on my life.

When God began to deal with my confidence, I went from feeling like my body was not enough to loving every part of me. At the same time, I began to love my internal self in a way I had never loved myself before. I began to acknowledge the brilliance within me including my thoughts, my personality, my abilities, and so much more beyond the achievements others had always praised me for.

One thing about this confidence journey is that it's one that is continuous. At every step of the journey, I've had to have renewed confidence. For example, with my body, I lose and gain weight from time to time and I have to be confident and choose to love myself through it. There are times when others make comments about my weight gain or how I look, and I have to fight within myself to choose me over their opinions. I have to align myself with the truth of God's Word that says I'm a beautiful masterpiece and that I am loved. Learning to love myself really allowed me to deflect everyone else's thoughts about me so that I could fully thrive and be my best self. Like I said, confidence is a decision and sometimes you have to make it daily even when you don't feel like it. Sometimes it's easier to side with what others say about you. If they say, "Wow you're big," sometimes it's easy to run to a mirror and say, "You know what… they're right… I am big."

Enough is enough. You have to draw a line in the sand and protect yourself and your confidence at all costs. Don't receive everything that others try to put on you and do your best to create boundaries to keep people's negative (and sometimes even innocent) thoughts away from you if it's going to deteriorate your confidence. You need to do what's best for you to maintain your confidence and sanity.

The world is always going to have some way of trying to tear you down, so fight to stay confident. How do you fight to stay confident? I'll share what works for me and what has worked for countless other women I coach. Fighting for your confidence includes a combination of prayer, journaling, and affirmations to build you up as opposed to tearing you down.

The more confident you are within, the more confident you are to make bold decisions and courageously step out of your comfort zone.

Just as much you need to have trust in God, I truly believe that you need to have the ability to trust yourself. You have to trust that God gave you everything you needed within you to succeed and defy the odds. Whenever you find yourself allowing logic to creep in, you have to remember that God has already equipped you for the journey ahead. You have countless talents and abilities and even some that you haven't tapped into yet.

Instead of talking yourself out of courageous moves of faith, I challenge you to talk yourself into it. One of the things that really helps me is to learn to start talking to myself the way that God talks to me. Over the years, you may have become accustomed to talking to yourself the same way that others have talked to you. For example, if people around you were condescending, rude, and mean, you may have talked down to yourself. If your thoughts about yourself and your behaviors tend to be negative, I challenge you to shift your thinking so that you can shift how you talk to yourself.

Positive self-talk will change your life. When nobody else is around to defend your confidence, you have to be willing to stand up for yourself and defend your confidence from within. You don't always have to verbally defend yourself against others' negativity, but you do have to take a moment to encourage yourself and remind yourself of the amazing human God created you to be.

When faced with fear, give yourself a positive talk and make that decision with faith. Trust that God will keep you safe, lead you, and position you to do things as courageous as walking on water.

Whether Jesus is calling you out to walk on water or it's your season to stand firm in what God already said, faith and confidence are both required. But now we're going to dip into a topic that many people struggle with as they are heading to thrive in their Promised Land. Let's talk about imposter syndrome.

# Dealing with Imposter Syndrome

What is imposter syndrome? Here's a note from a *Harvard Business Review* article by Gill Corkindale entitled "Overcoming Imposter Syndrome."[1]

> "Imposter syndrome can be defined as a collection of feelings of inadequacy that persist despite evident success. 'Imposters' suffer from chronic self-doubt and a sense of intellectual fraudulence that override any feelings of success or external proof of their competence. They seem unable to internalize their accomplishments, however successful they are in their field. High achieving, highly successful people often suffer, so imposter syndrome doesn't equate with low self-esteem or a lack of self-confidence. In fact, some researchers have linked it with perfectionism, especially in women and among academics."

Many high-achieving people struggle with imposter syndrome that comes from this idea of perfectionism. I used to struggle with it a ton, but it has become a lot more manageable now that I'm more aware of it. So, I'll speak from a place of experience and use "we". For those of us who struggle with imposter syndrome, we find that our perfectionism impacts our confidence. Though we may have fought to build up our self-esteem and confidence over the years, our desire to be perfect shifts our view of ourselves. Of course, we know that nobody is perfect, but we strive so often for the unrealistic

---

1. Gill Corkindale, "Overcoming Imposter Syndrome," *Harvard Business Review*, May 7, 2008, https://hbr.org/2008/05/overcoming-imposter-syndrome.

expectation of perfection, not just for ourselves, but for the work that we do and the roles that we play.

Of course, our Promised Land includes our careers, but it trickles down into our relationships with our families, our friends, our children, or our lovers. We pick ourselves apart because we don't focus so much on what was not perfect that we sometimes miss out on the beauty of what was amazing. We can all agree that something beautiful does not need to be perfect, but why do we continue to hold ourselves to this standard?

There are a few things that have helped me overcome moments of imposter syndrome. One thing is to talk to others who truly believe in me and have my best interest at heart. I remember there was one time when I was getting ready to take the stage at an event in Los Angeles in 2019. Right before going on stage to moderate the panel, I learned that a famous childhood actor would be on the panel and that her segment was being filmed for a major TV network. I almost panicked. Though I had taken the stage several times before and delivered great talks from the stage, I found myself questioning if I could make it happen on stage or if I'd crumble under the pressure. At that moment, I sent a text message to one of my closest friends explaining what was going on. He replied to me saying something along the lines of: "You were born for this. You've been doing this for a while, and you know what you're doing. This moment is everything aligning so you can walk in your calling." That was all I needed to take the stage with confidence instead of allowing imposter syndrome to make me crumble.

Another thing that really helps me deal with imposter syndrome is to pray and speak affirmations. Sometimes I find the nearest private place or bathroom to calm myself down before a big moment. Sometimes I stare at myself in the mirror and speak affirmations over myself affirming my abilities. Other times I may even put on soothing music like worship music or even some Beyoncé to shift my mood to focus on my brilliance and this amazing new opportunity I have to show up and walk in my brilliance. Instead of the moment seeming dreadful, I shift my perspective to see that this is a moment that I was born for, and I can walk in my calling according to it.

Here are forty of my favorite personal affirmations that I speak daily and even in tough moments when I realize imposter syndrome is trying to set in:

1. I am a multi-millionaire and billionaire.
2. I think like a billionaire.
3. I am brilliant, talented and worthy of success.
4. I am ridiculously creative and quick on my toes.
5. I am a powerful speaker with the power to shift an atmosphere with my words.
6. I trust that God leads me with my decisions and gives me discernment.
7. I am rich in wealth, resources, love, experiences, joy, faith, hope, and peace.
8. I do not allow negativity to phase me.
9. Everything I have need of always has provision.
10. I do not worry about anything, instead I pray about everything.
11. I am an amazing, supportive, loving, encouraging, faith-filled, praying, peaceful friend and human.

12. I have a sound mind even in chaos.
13. I fear no man nor woman and what they can do to me.
14. I am ridiculously wealthy.
15. Money flows to me easily.
16. I am a money multiplier.
17. I manage money well.
18. I immerse myself in luxury experiences because I deserve it.
19. I am loved. I deserve love.
20. I freely fall into the grace and mercy that God gives me daily.
21. My life impacts others greatly.
22. I am not hard on myself.
23. I give myself the grace to make mistakes.
24. I am a magnet for miracles.
25. An army of angels are always working on my behalf.
26. God is always moving even when I cannot see.
27. My body is beautiful.
28. Everything I touch turns to gold, including people.
29. I don't worry about who doesn't like me.
30. I continue to freely be myself wherever I go.
31. New money opportunities are drawn to me daily.
32. I am a high-paid speaker, coach, and business owner.
33. I can handle massive success with ease.
34. The more I give the more I receive.
35. I am in competition with nobody.
36. I make room for growth daily.

37. I celebrate my wins, even the small ones.
38. My life always points back to the goodness of God.
39. Every space I walk into is better because I was there.
40. I do not allow others to intimidate me out of walking in my purpose. I own and walk in my brilliance everywhere I go.

Affirmations may really help you a ton to re-center yourself and align with the truth of your existence and God's role in your life. Affirmations are a great way to become confident in moments when you don't feel it. Being confident in your abilities starts with acknowledging that you actually are pretty amazing. Not only are you amazing as a human being, but you have talent that really sets you apart from others. We all do. That's the beautiful thing about God. We all were created in His image, but he gave each of us a unique set of talents and even some that we have yet to explore.

Since many of us are recovering perfectionists and high-achievers, I believe it's important to pause and say that truly understanding yourself as a human has to come first before digging into your talents and achievements. For so long you may have identified yourself as a person who is honored for your accomplishments, but you are so much more than the abilities and talents that you bring to the table. Talents and abilities are admirable, but that's not the only thing that makes you phenomenal.

It's important to disassociate your abilities from your identity. Your talents do not make up who you are. Your essence and individuality is what makes you yourself. You are more than your talents and achievements. However, you should still acknowledge and own your unique talents and abilities.

Tapping into your unique talents requires that you own the fact that you are the bomb. You're the ish. Yes, I said it. You really are. I know if you picked up this book, you really are. What you're capable of doing is phenomenal. Chances are, you have way more than just one talent. It's okay to acknowledge that you are extremely talented and not feel bad or guilty that you have unique abilities.

When you're really walking in *Bold & Courageous* Confidence, you are allowing yourself to fully move past your past traumas, past hurts, the old view of yourself, and your fears, and instead choosing to walk with confidence. You are way more powerful than you could ever imagine. Make your daily decision to show up with confidence from that place.

I personally believe the best thing to ever back your decisions is the ability to hear God's voice and instructions clearly. In both Joshua and Abraham's situations, God spoke very clearly to both of them. Hearing God's voice isn't something that's just reserved for people who were in the Bible. We can hear God's voice on our own. John 10:27 CEV God states, "My sheep know my voice, and I know them. They follow me," and John 10:5 says: "The sheep will not follow strangers. They don't recognize a stranger's voice, and they run away."

Not only are we able to hear God's voice on our own, but we are also able to hear God's voice through others. There are many accounts in the stories of Joshua and Abraham where God spoke both directly to them and confirmed what He said through others. My situation was no different. God began to speak to me in my dreams, on billboards, on magazine covers, and through prophetic words. God's voice was not limited in my life.

I'll never forget that there was a time I was questioning whether I should leap out on faith and start with Epic Fab Girl. I was walking through an airport in San Jose, California. I'd ventured through this airport every single week for months and this day I saw a sign that was on the wall of a smoothie shop. The sign said "Go out on a limb. That's where the fruit is." That was my confirmation from God to fully step out on faith and take a chance at what He was speaking to me. That resonated with me not only because the message was great, but because God had already been speaking to me about stepping out on faith.

If you want to hear from God, you have to be intentional about silencing the noise in your life so that you can truly hear God's voice and His heart for you. When I was in my early twenties, I started to recognize the voice of God more clearly. Prior to that, I had been hearing God's voice ever since I was a kid, but I never thought I was really hearing from God. I did not recognize God's voice. I would have moments where things really resonated with me or something would drop in my spirit, but I could never really pinpoint a moment where I just knew God was speaking to me.

As I got older, I've been able to sharpen my ability to hear from God because I began to reflect on past moments when

I realized God was speaking to me. Once I recognized that, I was also able to be more intentional about hearing God's voice. Here are a few things that help me amplify God's voice in my life:

1. Fasting from food, social media, or TV

2. Reading and studying my Bible

3. Surrounding myself with other believers

Recognizing God's voice and instructions helps you to have another level of confidence. When you're walking in the confidence knowing that God has your back and that He's giving you the blueprint step by step, you can blaze trails you never thought possible. The best type of confidence to have is the kind where you know that God called you to live the life you're living. He gave you the talents He wants you to use, and He already has a plan for your life that is not only good, but it's victorious.

Don't shy away from owning your own brilliance. You deserve to shine. You deserve not to have to dim your light so that others can feel better about themselves.

# 9  *Bold & Courageous Conversations*

It takes courage to have hard conversations. It takes boldness to confront others when you need to have hard conversations. This chapter is dedicated to helping you still show up as your brilliant self even when you have to have bold and courageous conversations.

Deciding to have a hard conversation is healthy but it may also be tough to deal with. Especially if you're an over-thinker, like me, you may find yourself considering all the potential outcomes. I've learned that spending so much time mulling over potential outcomes can build unnecessary anxiety and stress leading up to conversations.

I used to be the person that avoided conflict and confrontation at all costs because I feared it escalating into an uncontrollable situation. The trauma of my past forced me to think of the ultimate worst situation happening, and I wanted to control outcomes in an effort to avoid tension and keep the peace. Sometimes that meant not speaking up for myself in moments I should have. I would find myself remaining quiet or convincing myself why this situation wasn't worth bringing up.

There were times when I talked myself out of having hard conversations, and eventually still had to have those hard conversations. It was usually worse off when I waited to confront issues because they'd been festering over time and really caused additional tension in the conversation that may not have been as intense had I discussed the conversation sooner.

The trouble with delaying an uncomfortable conversation is that you're choosing your own personal discomfort instead of speaking up. You're choosing to say that you prefer to cause yourself discomfort over causing discomfort to the other person(s) or the relationship. I think it comes down to an issue of valuing yourself enough to say that you deserve to have hard conversations that lead to bringing you more personal peace.

When you're having a hard conversation that impacts your overall well-being, you have to remind yourself that you deserve to have a tough conversation because you deserve true peace. I've learned that oftentimes hard conversations come when you need to enforce your personal boundaries or when someone has crossed a line you're not comfortable with them crossing. You deserve to speak up for yourself, no matter how awkward it may make you or the other person feel. Some of the best conversations I've ever had in life were difficult conversations I had that I chose not to back down from.

Hard conversations are not a bad thing. Hard conversations are healthy. I've had disagreements with friends and family over the years that have taught me the most about hard conversations. I've learned that leading with love is best while also inviting the Holy Spirit into the conversation. I've learned that saying what you really desire to say is what's most necessary and hearing the other person out is important, too. I've learned that those conversations can lead to healing, forgiveness, and less friction. There are times when you will have hard conversations that may shift the nature of your relationship with the person, but you have to be okay with choosing your own well-being and mental health over pleasing others.

If you struggle with having hard conversations, it could be directly linked back to the trauma that you've experienced over the years. Once you're aware of the ways that your past traumas impact your communication style with conflict and confrontation, it'll help you have healthier conversations. I've learned that it can be a good idea to be open and vulnerable with others letting them know that having a hard conversation is difficult for you. Sometimes when you open up to the other person and share how your past trauma impacts the way you communicate, it can help them have a better perspective on how to interact with you.

This goes beyond having hard conversations. I personally believe that those choosing to walk in their God-given authority should really position themselves to be self-aware and communicate to others how it impacts their interactions with others. I believe it's important to use discernment on who to open up that part of yourself with. The goal is to make sure that you open up to a safe person who you can trust and who will hear you out instead of passing judgment.

Some of the most difficult conversations to have will be with the people who caused you trauma. Let's be honest. Some of us have to interact and engage with those who have caused us trauma. Not everyone has the luxury of escaping the physical or relational proximity of the person who caused them harm. The truth is that it is our duty as Christians to forgive others for the pain they caused us, but having to interact with them can be difficult. More than likely, telling others how their behaviors negatively impact you currently or in the past will be hard. However, I've found that having those hard conversations may bring you peace, but you also have to be careful not to feel guilty for speaking up.

Your internal healing is essential for you to thrive in your Promised Land, and forgiveness is a huge part of that. I had to be extremely intentional about forgiving my parents because even as an adult, I desire to have a healthy relationship with both of them. Though my parents made many mistakes while raising me, they also did many things right. I love both of my parents very deeply and have been able to build healthier relationships with them as an adult, however it took work to get here. Forgiving others does not mean that you sweep everything that happened in the past underneath a rug to never be exposed again, rather you face the truth of what happened, forgive, and choose to move forward from it. When it comes to my parents, I refused to act as if what happened in my childhood never happened, but I also refused to allow their past mistakes to hinder any possibility of us having a healthy relationship in the future. Though I may not understand their decisions, I respect and love both of them, while still also being able to have hard conversations when it matters.

In my recent adult years, I've found great courage to be able to speak up and have open conversations with my parents about my upbringing. I've opened up and shared with them how their words and actions toward me impacted my life as a kid and my view of myself. I've often had to have those hard conversations on the back of my parents crossing a boundary that I wasn't comfortable with. As a child, my parents often spoke up about my body in a way that made me super self-conscious about it. I always had this constant reminder that I was the baby sister who was heavier than my sister that was two years older than me. I'd always be reminded that I had to shop in a special department for clothes that fit and reminded me of the constant frustration of trying to find things that fit my body somewhat appropriately.

As an adult, my parents continued that same liberty in discussing my body and it was hurtful. When I'd gain weight, they'd comment about it. When I lost weight, they'd be sure to emphasize that they thought I looked great and compliment me. Those conversations, for me, were extremely triggering. For a while I dealt with it, but eventually I had to speak up for myself otherwise I'd continue to be uncomfortable around them when they made statements about my body. I eased into the conversation with them to let them know that having conversations about my body and my health as an adult was my business and it was off limits for them to discuss. At first, you could tell they were offended and defensive, but I had to create a boundary that they had been continuously overstepping for years. As a kid I wasn't able to speak up for myself in this way, but as an adult, I owed myself the right to speak up and protect myself from unhealthy conversations so that I could have the healthy relationship I desire to have with my parents.

As I prepared to write this book, specifically, I knew I'd have to confront my parents about things in my childhood that remained family secrets for so long. Writing this book was one of the most bold and courageous things I've ever had to do. I had to be more raw and open than I had ever been before, placing my life on display so that others can learn, heal, and thrive. I even had to have tough conversations with my parents about how, though I love them very deeply, I would be sharing how growing up in the home with them impacted me as a child and now as an adult. It's hard to tell someone that you love and have forgiven that you're speaking out about your truth because it's going to help others heal. But this story was never about me. It has always been about God getting the glory and allowing you to also face your truth so that you, too, can heal.

Regardless of who you're having a hard conversation with, it's important to just do it. You have to face the hard conversations head-on and not back down from them. There's a way to peacefully communicate how you feel and your perspective without being disrespectful or tearing the other person down. Don't back away from asking the hard questions. Sometimes people will make you feel like you don't have the right to ask hard questions, but you do. Whether they want to answer or deflect is up to them. Bold and courageous conversations bring healing and often lead to restoration.

Your closest relationships are often some of the most difficult discussions to have, but I believe it's worth it to speak up if you desire to remain at peace with the other party in the long run.

Hard conversations often come after having to make a *Bold & Courageous* decision like the ones mentioned in chapter five. Whether you're breaking up with a romantic partner, choosing to let someone go at work, or deciding to cut ties with a friend, you may have to have a hard conversation. Don't beat yourself up for feeling the way you feel. You have the right to be entitled to your feelings.

Telling someone they hurt you is often difficult because it requires vulnerability. It may be easy to retreat to or default to defensiveness because you don't like being hurt or rejected. The healthy thing to do is speak up and share how you feel. The other person may not even know the level of harm they've caused you if you never speak up. You deserve to express how you feel, especially for those relationships that both parties are fully invested.

One of the most difficult conversations I've had to have was the one with me and the rest of the world about my experience being raped during college. For so long I remained silent about my experience, but when I chose to speak out about it, I felt nervous. I felt like I would be judged. I personally never decided to press charges against my assaulter, and for a long time, I felt guilty for not speaking up and protecting myself. Honestly, I didn't want to go through the pain of having to defend myself or prove to a judge that I was indeed wrongfully raped. The thought of that was extremely cringy and I wanted no parts with it. For the longest I allowed that piece of my story to silence me from speaking out. I felt like that discredited my experience because there was no legal proof that I was raped.

For many of us, there will come a time when we may have to speak out about our traumatic experiences. For some of us, we may even have to be vulnerable and share our traumatic experiences publicly. Regardless of how you decide to share, it's a courageous decision to speak up if you decide to. For me, personally, I knew that my decision to speak up about my experience would help others heal from their trauma. After originally sharing my experience with my audience on social media, I realized that many people suffer in silence about experiences because they feel alone and as if nobody will understand. It's a beautiful feeling to know that you are not alone.

I want you to remember that your story has power. Your story does not make you less than or unworthy. Your story is beautiful no matter how much trauma you've endured and no matter how much shame the world tried to spew your way. Your story has power, and I believe that you are called to share it with others, in some capacity, and it will change the trajectory of their lives. I encourage you to speak up and share your story because you have nothing to be ashamed about. You were called to walk in authority, shift atmospheres of every place you walk into, and impact generations for the glory of God. I believe it, and you should, too. Don't keep quiet because your story has the potential to change the world.

When I was raped in college, I didn't have the courage to speak up to friends and family until months or years after the experience. However, when I was raped years later, I took my power back by speaking up immediately and choosing to report the sexual assault to the police. I told my close family, friends, and even other believers I trusted. Having courageous conversations with friends, family, and the police really helped me to push through one of the most incredibly difficult seasons ever. Instead of feeling ashamed about what happened, I was able to feel empowered. Instead of bottling up all my emotions, I was able to get healing and freedom because I chose to speak up.

When traumatic things happen to us, the enemy wants us to believe that we are alone and powerless. The truth is that there is no promise that you won't ever experience negative situations, but God promises that He will be with you always. Here's the kicker: you maintain your power and authority through it all. I have learned to fight for my life from a place of spiritual warfare and trust that God has my back through it all. The same goes for you.

Regardless of the courageous conversation you need to have, whether it's with yourself, your family, your friends, your audience, or anyone else for that matter, remember to be bold in your approach. Your trauma does not define you, but it is a part of who you are.

> "And we know [with great confidence] that God [who is deeply concerned about us] causes all things to work together [as a plan] for good for those who love God, to those who are called according to His plan and purpose" (Romans 8:28 AMP).

Never forget that, just like God was with Joshua, He will always be with you.

# 10 *Bold & Courageous Perseverance*

What do you do when you feel like you're alone? What do you do when you feel like God's *not* there? The truth is this: as a trailblazer, you will experience moments when you feel alone and you feel like God's not there. You'll experience times when you feel like you're dealing with a series of unfortunate events and God's timing seems like cruel punishment. You'll be walking on the path of life God set for you and all of a sudden, your life will be in disarray, and you'll question if you're really on the right path to the Promised Land. This, my friend, is all a part of the promise.

According to the Merriam-Webster dictionary, perseverance is continued effort to do or achieve something despite difficulties, failure, or opposition. Your Promised Land requires perseverance as you face new battles and overcome new obstacles.

Leaders are often faced with so many challenges, both internally and externally. True leaders walk in authority no matter how much their authority is threatened and no matter how much life tries to intimidate them. Leaders persevere.

The year 2021 was a crazy year for me. I was hit with so many unexpected blows and being raped was at the top of that list. My life felt nearly perfect until this happened. When it happened, it felt like I was completely alone. It felt like God had abandoned me. It felt like God was not with me. All while I was dealing with fresh trauma, my business and life were shifting drastically. I had just returned from spending four months as a digital nomad in Mexico. When I left Mexico to avoid hurricane season, I thought I'd be returning after hurricane season was over. However, after I was raped while in Chicago, I was too nervous and anxious to live alone in Mexico anymore. My original plan completely shifted. I had to now figure out a plan for where to live the remainder of the year, and I had to sort out so much in my business. It felt like everything was hitting the fan.

I had sold my house a few months prior, and it was a complete struggle to find a new, safe place. I looked everywhere for a new apartment, but I kept getting rejected. It turns out that trying to get a place to stay as a full-time entrepreneur is a bit difficult because of proof of income and many other factors. I was annoyed and stressed out on top of hurting internally. I had zero strength. I was a walking zombie.

When it came to my business, I had to get rid of nearly my entire team. I lost tens of thousands of dollars in an effort to grow and scale my business. It seriously felt like a series of unfortunate events. I felt alone and abandoned by God.

I kept asking God questions like: "Where are you?" and "How are you in *this*?" I couldn't see Him. I couldn't feel Him the way I had in the past. It was weird and I was over it. I still showed up every Monday morning to pray for and pour into other women in my Epic Fab Girl community. God continued to show up in those spaces. I felt like I had been handed an extremely unfair hand of cards. How was I supposed to still push through and walk in purpose when I felt like I was being attacked on every front? How could I preserve through this when I felt alone?

I got to a point where I made a decision to step into my power. I made a decision to stop listening to the lies of the enemy that told me God *couldn't* be in this. I stopped questioning where God was, and I started shifting into utter and complete reliance on God.

Though I felt alone, I was not alone. Though I felt like God was not there, He *was* present. I had to remind myself of scriptures like, "[God] will never leave you nor forsake you" (Deuteronomy 31:6, NIV) and "If God is for us, who can be against us?" (Romans 8:31, NIV).

When I was raped, I had just completed writing this book. I had found myself having to literally walk through another major moment in life where I, too, had to be *Bold & Courageous*.

The funny thing is that we often hear about how God will never leave nor forsake you, but we omit the full verse. Deuteronomy 31:6 NIV says: "Be strong and courageous. Do not be afraid or terrified because of them, for the Lord your God goes with you; he will never leave you nor forsake you". I didn't even notice this until I had to walk through it on my own and pull on the Word of God for my strength.

Here I was, yet again, met with the reminder to be *Bold &
Courageous* because God *was* with me.

As I said, I had just written this book, and it felt like a major
struggle to finalize the process. I had no desire to publish it. I
was in so much pain, but I now realize that the book needed
an alternate ending. Sometimes your pain will birth the most
beautiful parts of your purpose.

You may think that perseverance always looks like a fight,
but I'd argue that perseverance often looks like complete and
total surrender. It looks like saying "yes" to God and "yes"
to your purpose one day at a time. It looks like letting go of
everything that you thought your Promised Land journey
would look like. It looks like letting God do what God does
to "fix" things instead of trying to do it on your own. That's
what it looked like for me.

Yes, there will be times when you have to persevere by fighting, but that's not always the requirement.

So, what do you do when you feel like you're alone? You
remind yourself that you are not alone and that God is always
with you.

What do you do when you feel like God's not there? You
remind yourself that He is. He's omnipresent and He knows
exactly everything you've endured.

I'm no theologian, and I cannot explain why we go through
pain, suffering, and struggles. However, I can tell you that
many great people in the Bible had to endure hard times to get
to their Promised Land. Think Noah, Abraham, Sarah, Moses,

Joseph, Gideon, Shadrach, Meshach, Abednego, David, Mary, and Joseph… the list could go on. I can tell you just how James (the brother of Jesus) said it in James 1:2-4 NIV:

> "Consider it pure joy, my brothers and sisters, whenever you face trials of many kinds, because you know that the testing of your faith produces perseverance. Let perseverance finish its work so that you may be mature and complete, not lacking anything."

What if your trials were built to grow your faith and ability to persevere? What if they were built just for you to surrender to God and trust God *more*? It takes real faith to stand in the midst of the worst things you've ever experienced and still say, "God, I trust you."

Is perseverance easy? No. But, I can tell you from personal experience, that it gets easier the more you surrender. It gets easier when you shift your mind from a place of defeat to a place of victory. It gets easier when you remember that God is on your side and there is nothing that's too hard for Him.

When I found myself in what felt like a pit in 2021, I leaned on God, and I leaned on my Courage Circle. Your Courage Circle is a group of people who you can count on. These are trusted advisors, friends, and peers who will not judge you. These are people who are able to see you the way God sees you and will not place you on a pedestal. These people recognize your humanity and will not use what they know about you to tear you down or for their own personal gain. Developing your Courage Circle is key because these are the people who you can run to in times of crisis, weakness, and struggle.

During that time, I had good days and I had bad ones. I had days when I felt like my faith was on 1,000, but there were days when I felt my faith was depleted. In those moments, that's when I was able to lean on God and lean on my Courage Circle to encourage me and pray for me.

I, then, got to a place of total surrender. I gave up on looking for a new apartment, and I spent some time in Los Angeles to meet with a client and to also take a breather. While I was in Los Angeles, God gave me specific instructions on where to look for a new apartment. I searched and found the perfect apartment, but my application was rejected in the final stages of the process. I felt bummed, but I kept following God's instructions. I kept searching, and a real estate agent helped me find a place, but it wasn't exactly what I was looking for. I prayed about it and didn't feel peace about moving forward with it, so I told her that I'd pass. A few days later, she reached out with a new apartment for me to see that had everything I wanted (except a pool). This place was in an even better location than the first place I thought was perfect.

In a matter of seven days total, I found a new apartment I loved, got it nearly fully furnished amidst a national furniture shortage, and moved in. At first, it felt like my back was against the wall, but God was there every step of the way. God suddenly shifted everything, made a way out of no way, and provided me with a fresh, new miracle. But here's the thing, the shift was going to happen regardless, and I had to trust that He would do exactly what He said He would do.

One of the things that I love about the story of Joshua's leadership with the Children of Israel in the Bible is that God did not give Joshua the full plan upfront. As Joshua obeyed God, He gave him more and more instructions. Joshua had to trust that God would provide instructions along the way and equip him with everything he needed to be successful.

Sometimes there will be times when you have to fight a battle with God's leading. Other times there will be moments when you need to stand still and allow God to fight for you to redeem and vindicate you.

Perseverance is required when you're going through personal attacks in your own life, but also in your career and with your influence.

It can be difficult to just sit back and allow yourself to be attacked or even ridiculed and criticized. I find that this is the time when the wounds of past traumas and items in the Bold Room like to rear their ugly heads. What happens when you feel like your back is against the wall and the enemy is attacking you? Or what about what happens when someone spreads lies about your name? What happens when someone else calls your leadership and decisions into question when you are not in the wrong? Do you fight back with your words or even physically? Or do you crumble under the pressure?

The reality is that if God is calling you higher and elevating your platform, you will be visible for others to see. Chances are that your success and actions will be on display for others to see. Everybody won't be a fan of you, which is why it's so important to overcome the need to please others. There is no way that you will be liked by everyone. If you think about it, there are people who criticize so many legends like Michelle

Obama, Beyoncé, Priscilla Shirer, and Oprah, to name a few. If phenomenal women and heroes like these women are criticized, we know nobody is off-limits for others who cannot see you the way that God sees you.

Every leader will go through ups and downs. There are moments when there are victories and there are moments when you will be attacked. There are moments when you will be celebrated, and there will be moments when you are criticized. It's the world we live in and it's the life that God called you to. That's exactly why it's extremely important to follow God and obey what He says to do.

A true leader rises to the occasion and does not take every chance they get to defend themselves. They persevere and focus on the path to the Promised Land. Oftentimes our unhealed trauma can cause us to act out of character, causing us to put all we have worked for on the line. You know it's not worth it, but it can take a lot of convincing in a heated moment when you feel like you need to defend yourself.

I personally believe that it's extremely important to implement an ongoing healing plan in your life to make sure that you maintain your healing. I also believe it's important to continuously spend time fasting, praying, journaling, and seeing a professional counselor or therapist. Leaders have a unique road they must follow and it's not always easy, so it's important to have people and systems in place prior to moments when you may feel like you're in a crisis.

At work, leaders are often tasked with making hard decisions that can lead your business or workplace down an unexpected path. No matter how calculated you may get, there's no real way to make decisions that will have expected outcomes every single time. Life has so many variables that can impact the outcomes of a situation. When it comes to making decisions in the workplace, you have to learn to commit to your decisions without spending too much time overthinking them. I have personally learned that putting a decision-making process in place helps me to make decisions even when I'm faced with difficult ones.

Leaders make mistakes, too. When you're taking risks and moving quickly, you will make mistakes. Not every risk you take is going to yield phenomenal results, and you have to live with that, too. The key is to allow yourself the grace to get things wrong and speak up about your mistakes when necessary. I believe that the best leaders are open about their struggles, mistakes, and shortcomings. Whether it's making a business decision or a life decision that impacts others negatively, I believe that leaders should speak out about it.

True leaders take accountability and apologize when they're wrong. Making a mistake makes you human. Hiding and covering up your mistakes can make you a villain. One of the most beautiful outcomes of making mistakes is building trust with others who are under your leadership or within your realm of influence. It takes major guts to say that you were wrong and own up to your mistakes. Doing this helps you stand out from the crowd and builds trust with your sphere of influence.

Of course, you may be judged for the way you make decisions. You may also be judged for how you handle your mistakes. But this is why I have said time and time again that having a real relationship with God, a professional therapist, and a circle of trusted friends and mentors will be extremely beneficial in your journey into and through the Promised Land. There will be moments when you feel like you can't deal with the weight or the pressure of your calling, and this is when your Courage Circle comes into play. They help you persevere.

Hard conversations are not only necessary for you to initiate with others, but it's important to be open to hard conversations from those in your Courage Circle, specifically. Nobody is perfect, and neither are you. I believe that in order to walk in the full authority that God has given you, you must remain humble, be open to correction, and find a safe space within your Courage Circle.

Your character shapes your ability to persevere through tough times. Courageous leaders exude kindness and vulnerability while also remaining firm in their approach. Courageous leaders have taken the time to heal from their past, restore their view of themselves, and learn to lead with love. Unhealed leaders often use their superiority to fill voids to account for their insecurities or unhealed traumas. For example, if you've ever worked for someone who was extremely hard on you or spoke condescendingly toward you, chances are they have unhealed trauma from their past. It may not always be that they're speaking down to you because they don't like you, but rather they are conditioned to speak to others and themselves harshly.

This is why it's key to be kind to yourself and learn to have positive self-talk. Leaders will treat others the same way they treat themselves. Courageous leaders treat everyone with the same level of respect, regardless of if the other person has any impact on their life or not. It's important to treat others well regardless of if you can gain something from them or not. Bold leaders create a culture of transparency, forgiveness, kindness, and make room for making mistakes. I believe that these are some of the major ingredients to building a character that helps you persevere.

Ultimately, to persevere through adversity and life's crazy, winding path to the Promised Land you must possess love, joy, peace, longsuffering, kindness, goodness, faithfulness, gentleness, and self-control. These are the fruit of the Spirit according to Galatians 5:22-23 NKJV.

When mistakes happen, it's not the end of the world. While some mistakes may be costly, it's never worth the cost of demeaning or talking down to others or yourself. To be a trusted leader, you must speak only to build others up and never to tear people down. This is one of my own personal life mantras.When I first entered corporate America I had a manager, Rick, who was very fond of me. He was always looking out for me and wanted to see me succeed at the firm. I was interested in chatting with other leaders in the company to gain an understanding of what type of projects I'd be interested in for the future. So, Rick connected me with another leader, Justin, who was pretty high up in the company. My manager, Rick, coordinated a coffee chat with the three of us and I was pretty nervous the entire time. I wasn't really sure what to expect from the conversation, so I came with questions and thought I did a pretty good job holding my own and getting to know Justin. During the entire meeting, I thought my manager, Rick, was pleased with my performance.

As soon as we left the meeting, Rick politely pulled me to the side. He first asked me if I was open to a coaching moment. I said, "Sure." He began to give me feedback on my interaction with Justin and how I should be better prepared for it in the future. I received the feedback well. Even though the message he was delivering was not necessarily positive, at no time did I feel disrespected or demeaned. I felt coached to improve on my performance in the future and it felt like a very fruitful conversation. I did not feel like I was a failure simply because of how he approached me. I later went on to build a solid relationship with Justin and was able to do a major presentation in front of him and several executives at a Fortune 100 Company. I'll never forget how Justin congratulated me for holding my own and was really impressed with my presentation.

Mistakes happen. It's all a part of the process. It's your job to persevere even when you make mistakes. Don't feel defeated when you make mistakes, rather, grow from them and keep it pushing.

Outside of the world of corporate America, there are leaders who position themselves as an authority online, like me. Many of these leaders make mistakes often, too. It amazes me how often other leaders and experts use their platforms to diminish, demean, and criticize others who have made mistakes. I personally believe that the most courageous leaders are the ones who don't spend time using their platform to tear others down, rather they use their platform to uplift and spread the truth. Many leaders may make decisions and mistakes that cause their public platform to take a hit or completely crumble, but we must remember these leaders and experts are human, too. We must remember that we should extend the same grace that we wish to receive from others if we were in their shoes. My rule of thumb is no different than what I was taught as a kid, "If you don't have anything nice to say, don't say anything at all."

You never know when you'll be the leader that's up on the chopping block for your decisions. Whether it's a scandal, slander, or a major public failure. There's no guarantee that you can avoid any of the above, but you can persevere through it. Whether you believe in karma or the thought that "what goes around comes around," it may be in your best interest to treat others the way you want to be treated. I've learned that when you tend to extend grace to others, others will extend grace to you. However, if you've been extremely harsh to others, people will tend to repay you with the same level of intensity that you've treated others.

Sometimes you may be up against a situation where you are not in the wrong. Sometimes your words may be twisted up against you or lies may be told about you. But bold leaders speak from a place of courage and truth. Even if you look at the story of Joseph in the Bible, Potiphar's wife lied on Joseph saying that he tried to sexually assault her. This lie caused Joseph to be placed in jail for years even though he told the truth. But we already know that leaders may have to persevere through situations that others may not be able to deal with. Joseph had to pay the sacrifice of speaking truth, but it was the Lord who redeemed him, eventually. Joseph continued to speak the truth and persevered through prison to eventually become a high-ranking leader who broke generational curses through his obedience to God.

Joseph's story in the Bible is a key example of God's faithfulness and redemption in our lives. It's an extremely powerful story that emphasizes the power of forgiveness, longsuffering, and perseverance. Joseph endured so much trauma as a child with his jealous siblings hating him and throwing him into a pit. He was sold into slavery and eventually became the second most high-ranking leader in Egypt after many years. The story goes that when there was a great famine in the land where his brothers were, they were forced to come to Egypt to receive food. When Joseph recognized his brothers, he had to make a decision to bless them. Instead of holding onto bitterness, Joseph wept privately and was able to bless his brothers and family, letting go of what happened to him as a child. Had he not persevered through tough times, Joseph would have never been able to help his family in that way.

We can learn something very significant from Joseph. True courageous leaders not only forgive, but they make room for others to thrive no matter how they've been treated by them. Courageous leaders position others to thrive and receive blessings. Having a healed heart is intensely important because you do not want your past hurt to impact the future that God has for you. For you to be a true instrument of God to advance God's Kingdom, you will have to let go of your past so you can walk in your Kingdom assignment.

I'll never forget one of my first women managers in corporate America, Sunita. I was working on a project that was based in Silicon Valley, which was one of the best projects I'd ever experienced. My manager was an Indian woman who taught me so much about being *Bold & Courageous*. She required excellence from her team but also had the ability to be forgiving. She meant serious business, and I loved how she stood her ground even when others criticized her leadership. I learned a lot from Sunita about being a force to be reckoned with. I remember sitting in rooms with her when we would be at a table full of executives, and we would be the only two women in the room. Sometimes I'd look up and I would be the only person under thirty years old, only black person, and one of two women in the room. It was hard to walk into those rooms at times and feel like I belonged there, but Sunita's presence in meetings always reminded me that I did.

We had been working on a huge project for a few months and it was time to present our findings and what we had been working on to leadership. Sunita told me that she wanted me to present our research to leaders and I was so scared. It was literally my very first year in corporate America and here I was this twenty-four-year-old black girl from Chicago who was tasked to present to a group of about twenty executives that included vice presidents of organizations from our client's side and several high-level executives from our consulting firm. Of course, I took on the challenge and felt confident that I'd mastered the art of giving business presentations in my MBA program. I was seriously scared, though. I really knew my stuff about this project. I'd been working on it day in and day out for the past few months. One of the things that really helped me overcome fear in that moment was when I realized that Sunita trusted me to present so I knew I could rise to the occasion. I went into the presentation, and I did so well. The presentation was phenomenal, relatable and I got so many raving reviews from the executives, including Justin who I had previously connected with. I was amazed and it really helped me build my confidence.

I often think back to that situation and recall that Sunita had the ability to give the presentation herself, but she didn't. She gave me my moment to shine by making room for me and giving me an opportunity that would present me extremely well in front of our clients and colleagues. Sunita's decision to trust me was a bold and courageous move. She could have easily allowed pride to get in the way by taking the platform to present, but she didn't. She was never one of the leaders who just took all the credit for the work that was being done behind the scenes. She let me show up as a stakeholder and helped me be taken seriously by others regardless of my entry-level role in the company. She taught me such a major lesson that I'll never forget.

Bold, courageous leaders are not prideful. Yes, you are talented. Yes, you are blessed. However, pride will become your demise if you let your decisions be made with pride. God's Word instructs us to be humble and avoid prideful spirits. If we are not careful, our unhealed trauma can cause us not to remain humble in our actions.

I don't care what anybody says, but true *Bold & Courageous* leaders are humble. PERIOD. Humility is key. Lack of humility can cost you. Proverbs 16:18 NIV states, "Pride goes before destruction, a haughty spirit before a fall." I know you can think of someone for who this verse rings true. Humility is so essential as a leader and as a trusted expert. Humility, honesty, transparency, and openness are key to becoming an authority who can be trusted.

One of the major ways that trailblazers can persevere as leaders is through prayer. Bold and courageous leaders not only lead well, but they're vulnerable and pray for the people they're leading and influencing. You can pray for your team and audience publicly or privately, but I've learned that leading into business meetings with prayer, when possible, really allows room for my meetings to flow more smoothly. Prayer invites God into your workplace and allows for more vulnerability even among your team and audience. I believe that sharing vulnerable moments causes you to be viewed as more human and helps your team become more receptive and open to you.

For example, when I'm struggling to make a decision or having a rough time, I do not keep that from my team. I'm open with them and allow them to know that I'm having a moment and that I'm not perfect. It takes courage to open up to others to allow them to see you even in moments when you're not feeling your strongest. It creates a culture that is not harsh and allows for others to experience grace and freely give it because of the culture you create. It also helps you persevere. I made the courageous decision to open up to my team about the sexual assault I experienced in 2021 while I was going through it. I opened up in an effort to show them my humanity, but it also created space for them to support me in ways I didn't realize.

This was a bold decision for me because I did not know how they would respond or treat me. Every single person on my team was kind, understanding, and allowed me the space to heal as I took very necessary mental health days. My team was able to step up to the plate and take more onto their plates because my capacity was so low for quite some time.

The truth is that life happens, and we cannot control the problems that we go through or the timing. Walking in your true God-given authority means that you show up as a leader, but you don't neglect your humanity. You are not a superhero, and you don't want to create unrealistic expectations for how to show up at work when life gets tough.

Perseverance can be difficult, but you have to expect your need for it. The road to success is not a straight, smooth path. You'll need to have tools in your arsenal to persevere through tough times, but never forget that you should count it all joy when you face trials and tribulations.

You may be wondering how in the world can you be joyful in the face of adversity. I'm a living witness that when you surrender your life and your plans to God you will be able to find joy in the midst of your trials and tribulations. Trials are just a sign to remind you that you're on the right path and that God is standing with you, even when it doesn't feel like it. He's there, so just hold onto your faith and know that the same God who redeemed you before and created miraculous moments for you before can do it again. Better yet, He can do it in a brand-new way and blow your mind.

God may be coming to your rescue in a new way, so don't miss Him. Just trust that He's with you and that your job is to be *Bold & Courageous* no matter what you're up against.

You were born with your God-given authority. God created you for this journey. You will always need to actively work on refining your leadership, character, and ability to persevere, but you must be intentional about it. You will gain success on your journey, so do not be afraid to make risky decisions and be open and honest with those you're influencing and leading.

## Here are a few questions to reflect on to move forward:

1. What fruit of the Spirit do you need to work on building?

2. How can you show up in a more vulnerable way?

3. Who is in your Courage Circle?

4. What is your course of action when you and your decisions are being attacked?

# 11 *Bold & Courageous Authority*

Ever since my mother birthed me, the enemy has made every attempt to try to make me dim my light. From being dubbed the "golden child" by my siblings, to walking the harsh hallways of Beasley in fourth grade, to dealing with betrayal with friends and romantic relationships throughout my life... the list could go on for a while. The enemy's goal was to make me view myself differently than God viewed me. If I'm honest, the enemy's plan worked... almost. While the enemy's plan tried to settle in and take root, there was nothing that God couldn't shift in my life. I mean, after all, God is the one who created the plan for my life and uniquely molded me to be the perfect fit for it.

For a long time, I dimmed my light. I walked into rooms as if I was less than and unworthy. I entered relationships as if I was not enough and as if I was not the prize. I settled for less than in many situations because I was convinced that I did not deserve better. There were many moments when I, both consciously and subconsciously, believed something different than the truth of what God had to say about me. That's exactly what influenced my decision to dim my light.

God is the source of your light, so the enemy cannot dim the light. The enemy's plan is to intimidate you to the point of choosing to dim your light so that you can show up as a settler. He wants you to settle into a personality, lifestyle, and path that was never meant for you.

Here's what I want you to remember: you are the one who has access to the switch that controls how you bring your light to the world. The enemy cannot control your light. You have a choice when it comes to how you show up. You can either show up in the fullness of the bright light that God gave you. Or you can choose to show up as a dimmer, less authentic version of yourself in order to please others or out of fear of what others will say.

I know you may be thinking that this sounds easier said than done. You may even be wondering how to stop dimming your light after spending so many years showing up as a less authentic version of yourself. Here's my simple answer: just walk in it. Yes, I believe it takes work and practice, but you have to simply start by showing up with your full light shining, one decision at a time.

> "You are the light of the world. A town built on a hill cannot be hidden. Neither do people light a lamp and put it under a bowl. Instead they put it on its stand, and it gives light to everyone in the house. In the same way, let your light shine before others, that they may see your good deeds and glorify your Father in heaven" (Matthew 5:14-16 NIV).

God gave you the authority. It's yours to walk in. It's already there for you to claim. Walk in the authority that God gave you. Period. What's the authority that God gave you? Let's look at Romans 8:11 NIV: "And if the Spirit of him who raised Jesus from the dead is living in you, he who raised Christ from the dead will also give life to your mortal bodies because of his Spirit who lives in you."

God has given you authority and power through the Holy Spirit. The same Holy Spirit that raised Jesus from the dead is *alive* in you. I want you to picture yourself making decisions and showing up everywhere you go with the same power that raised Jesus from the dead. It may be hard to believe or picture, but that's the reality if you've accepted Jesus Christ as your Lord and Savior. You have that power. It's already within you, so all you have to do is tap into it. Just flip the switch.

Now here's one of the hardest parts. Many people say that you're your own worst critic, but it doesn't have to be that way. I want you to shift from being your own worst critic to being your biggest fan on earth. If God created a magnificent plan for your life and created you to fulfill it, you cannot tell me that He's not your #1 fan in the universe when it comes to *His plan* for your life. Not only do I want you to walk in your God-given authority, but I also want you to treat yourself nicely in the process.

Let's talk about being nice to yourself. For many years, I was not nice to myself at all. I was hard on myself. I spoke negatively about myself, my accomplishments, and my body. I had been conditioned to believe that I was not enough, so I spoke to myself in a way that exemplified my beliefs. I would say things (out loud and in my head) like, "You'd look even better with a flat stomach," or "You talk too much." I'd say things like that because I heard others say it about me and somewhere along the way I started to believe them. So, to avoid others' negativity, I shifted myself and my view of myself in an attempt to be better received by the world. But what was the result? A less authentic version of myself which meant that the world was missing out on the fullness of my greatness and brilliance.

We previously talked about the Bold Room that may be cluttered with baggage and residue from trauma. Let's revisit the Bold Room to help you move forward. The Bold Room has many things within it that may have caused you to speak down to yourself and be mean to yourself. Maybe your family was tough on you. Maybe you were molested, and you blame yourself for it. Maybe you were cheated on and you beat yourself up for not seeing the signs. Maybe, like me, you were raped and immediately felt like it was your fault because of your decisions that led up to being taken advantage of. Maybe you pardoned your abuser and grew closer to your abuser over time. I don't know what's in your Bold Room, but I do know that you don't have to talk down to yourself about what's in (or was in) there. It takes time to unlearn these behaviors, but I want you to make an effort to be nice to yourself and treat yourself with kindness. Anytime you find yourself going down a path of negativity, I want you to backpedal and cover your tracks with positivity.

How can you show up to the world in the fullness of your authority if you're not nice to yourself, first?

A true *Bold & Courageous* authority shows up confidently and unapologetically in their brilliance. They acknowledge their imperfections while also harnessing the power they possess to impact the world beyond belief. I believe every trailblazer has the capability to shift atmospheres, change generations, and make riveting impacts on society. Becoming the highest version of yourself is essential to make that happen. This version of you is ever evolving, so you have to be willing to change and adapt for the better.

You are an authority. It's within you. It's time to stop apologizing for your brilliance. It's time to stop saying "I'm sorry" for no reason at all. Remove those words from your vocabulary unless you are really in a moment of apologizing. It may be easy to just cut "I'm sorry" out the picture if you replace it with "I apologize". Some of us have been so conditioned to say "I'm sorry" when we get things wrong because we are expecting perfection and feel bad for getting things wrong. We are human. We are going to make mistakes. Some mistakes require an apology while others don't.

For example, you're at work and you missed an important deadline because you were swamped with work. That's definitely a time to apologize because you did not play your part and you can admit fault. However, let's say you had an emergency with your family that caused you to miss an important deadline at work. You communicated that you'd miss the deadline ahead of time because your family life takes priority over work life. In this case, there's no need to apologize because you're literally a human who had a family situation come up that was outside your control. You can easily communicate with your team that you had a family emergency, and you have to go offline.

Some people believe that you cannot be considered an authority or expert unless you've put in countless hours for multiple years. I believe that thought is misleading because if we pay attention to how quickly the world and technology evolve around us, we can understand that someone can gain expertise in an area in a short period of time. While I believe that spending years doing something does add to your expertise, it is not a requirement to develop expertise in something. For example, there are infants that know how to work a smartphone better than some adults. Children are quick learners and master tasks quickly, and we should have that same understanding of adult ability. You can learn from anybody. Anybody can learn from you.

# 11.1 *Walking in Authority in Your Career*

In my book, to be considered an expert or authority, you must have depth of knowledge and understanding in the area of focus of your expertise. Here are a few examples to display my definition of expertise:

1. Lily worked closely with celebrities doing crisis management for two years. She worked on multiple high-profile cases to manage crises and created public relations campaigns around them. Though Lily has only done this work for two years, she can be considered an expert in crisis management for celebrities and others looking for the same outcomes.

2. Jason has been working as an administrator for fifteen years in a medical records office. Though he has no certification to back his expertise, he can be considered an expert in productivity, organization, and medical administrative work.

3. LaKisha spent a year living in Ghana studying Ghanaian culture to conduct research. She received

an award for her research from Ghanaian leaders and leaders from her home country. She can be considered an expert in the specific area of focus within her research.

4. Brian has been building websites and designing brand logos for seven years. He has not received any awards or accolades to be featured in major magazines or publications, however his clients give him raving reviews.

Each of these cases showcase the individual's expertise. While they may not know everything, they definitely can be considered an authority within an area of focus or a niche. Each person is considered an expert and has high value to society. Experts do not claim to know *everything*, rather they claim to have expertise in a specific area. Your expertise gives you the authority to consider yourself an expert.

You can consider yourself an expert if you have learned and mastered something and are able to teach others about it. Oftentimes we may discount our expertise, knowledge, and abilities because we feel we do not know everything. That's exactly why there's so much power in honing in on your area of focus within your expertise.

It's difficult to say you know everything on a specific topic, but it's more palatable and reasonable to say that you have researched a niche and have become a trusted person of value within that area of focus.

For example, I have been building a business officially since 2011. Prior to that, I had small side hustles and websites that

I launched to showcase work that I'd done. At the time of writing this book, I have officially been an entrepreneur with an established business for ten plus years. While I know a lot about business strategy and I'm extremely creative, I own a specific area of expertise: digital marketing for service-based businesses and digital product owners. I've mastered the worlds of email marketing, developed strategies that work well for myself and my clients on Instagram, with SMS marketing, and other forms of digital marketing. There's so much value in being able to say that I have an area of focus and I choose to be open and transparent as I tell others that I do not have expertise in other areas. For example, if someone comes to me and wants me to share a strategy for them that would help them make massive profits as a product-based business owner on Amazon, I would not feel comfortable giving them a strategy. That's not my area of expertise and I have not studied how to be effective with marketing on Amazon. I do, however, continue to learn, grow, and receive training in the areas that I have developed my expertise in.

It takes courage and humility to tell others that you are not an expert in a specific area even if they desire you to be. There may be times where someone may come to you requesting your help in an area simply because it sounds similar to your area of expertise. However, in cases that what they're looking for isn't within your wheelhouse, you should comfortably speak up and let them know that it's not something you'd be able to help with. No need to apologize either. Instead of saying, "I'm sorry I can't help you. I wish I could help," you could instead say, "I wish I could have been more help to you, but my area of expertise is in (fill in the blank)." It's okay not to know everything, and there should never be an expectation for you to know everything. You should not be presenting to the world that you know everything and never get anything wrong.

Now let's get into stepping into and walking in your brilliance and authority. You already know that you are the bomb. If you're reading this book, I want to remind you that you are. You are ridiculously gifted and talented. You have the ability to transform the world beyond belief. Your influence is massive and unlimited. Your gifts will continue to make room for you.

As an authority, you have to learn to step into your brilliance. Do not back down or shy away from it. Sometimes we may work so hard to be viewed as humble so we don't speak up in moments when we could allow for our brilliance to be on display. Just because you're humble, that doesn't mean that you have to keep your mouth shut about your abilities and expertise.

If you have accolades and accomplishments that are noteworthy, that's even more of a reason to consider yourself an authority. However, you have to see yourself as an authority before anybody else can. If you cannot see that you really are phenomenal at what you do, you will always back down and cower in the face of even the scariest moments.

Don't be afraid to stand in your authority. Don't be afraid to position yourself as an authority online.

Positioning yourself as an expertise means that you open your mouth to share your expertise. This could mean that you begin creating content and sharing your research online. This could also mean that you start posting information online on social media to educate an audience on your area of focus. This could be taking on projects in your area of expertise that showcase your ability. Experts show up as thought leaders by sharing information, solving complex problems, and challenging societal norms. Don't be afraid to speak out because, eventually, you will be viewed as an authority. It requires consistency to speak out within the area of your expertise. The more you show up, the more chances others have the ability to see your expertise.

One of the major ways I see true experts discounting their abilities is around pay. Whether it's in a corporate setting or in entrepreneurship, I've learned that many experts initially settle for getting paid less than they deserve because they do not recognize the weight of their gift and experiences. They don't recognize the true authority they have. I've often realized, especially for the women that I coach in business, that what experts initially charge or demand to be paid is tied to their own personal self-worth and value. Though they may recognize that their work is valuable, they cannot bring themselves to be comfortable enough to demand getting paid premium prices. They often do this because they may feel guilty about assigning a high value to their work, which, in their minds, is tied to their self-worth. When you walk in authority, one must do the difficult work of removing those negative mindsets about pay so that they can receive the abundance and blessings that their gifts will allow for.

When you transition from settling for what others offer you into owning your value, expertise, and authority, you can begin to negotiate better terms for your pay and other benefits. I've learned that many people settle for less than what they deserve not because they always believe they deserve less, but rather because they do not feel confident and worthy enough to ask for what they truly deserve. A *Bold & Courageous* authority is willing to negotiate for what they deserve and is willing to walk away from opportunities that do not align with the level of brilliance and expertise they bring to the table.

# 11.2 *Walking in Spiritual Authority*

The Bold Room is the place where many of your deepest, darkest secrets once lived. The more you evaluate what's in your Bold Room and clear out space for what was always meant to be, the more you can walk in your God-given calling, abilities, and authority.

As a woman who has experienced so much trauma in my life, at one point it had become so difficult to see myself as an authority or expert. I have to fight for my confidence daily in moments when the world tries to bully me out of my calling. There are moments when negativity tries to creep in from others to cause me to fall off track, and I've learned to take time to build myself back up in the Word of God and to immerse myself in things and people that make me feel most alive. It's normal to feel like you are scared to move forward, to get started, or to finish, but that's why it's so important to have a Courage Circle to help you through the journey.

Every moment I've experienced over the years from the trauma of being teased as a young kid, to witnessing domestic violence in my home, to being betrayed by my closest friends as a teenager, to experiencing rape and heartbreak as an adult... it all impacted me in some sort of way. Nothing was too hard for God to heal, but I also had to be intentional in my healing process so I could step into the fullness of my calling and authority. Of course, there are times when I'm scared or when I feel unsure of my decisions, but I am fully convinced that God will be with me every step of the way.

I am able to confidently and unapologetically walk in my God-given authority because I know that this is the life that God called me to. I know this is the space He called me to occupy in the world and that no devil in hell nor human on earth can block what God destined for my life. The same thing goes for you.

You, my friend, are a *Bold & Courageous* authority. The world is waiting for you to unleash the possibilities within you. The world is waiting on your brilliance to illuminate our lives and our minds. You are phenomenal and there's no way you should back down. You are not who you once were. Leave old things in the past, allow God to heal you and renew your mind. It's time to take bold steps of faith in the direction of your purpose.

• • •

When the enemy tries to intimidate you out of your God-given authority, remind yourself that you were built for this. The enemy wants to destroy you. But never forget that God gives us the power to overcome all the powers of the enemy and remain unharmed (Luke 10:19).

Remind yourself that you already have the authority to stand up against the enemy and wage war from a place of victory. Remind yourself that God is with you every step of the way.

Being *Bold & Courageous* doesn't mean that you'll never be afraid. Being *Bold & Courageous* means that you're not willing to give up or back down. It means that you'll walk in the authority God gave you despite what life throws your way. Being *Bold & Courageous* takes daily decisions, but I know you've got it in you to live boldly and courageously show up as the beautiful human God created you to be.

May you hang onto the words of this book as a reminder that God has your back and that God can bring beauty from ashes to restore you even when you think your life is unsalvageable. May you walk forward with power and authority and be reminded that you have it in you to be *Bold & Courageous*.

As I close this book, my final words are a prayer for you.

*Dear Heavenly Father,*
*I pray that every word of this book has penetrated the heart*
*and mind of this special reader as you designed. I pray that*
*as each reader walks forward in destiny, that you will be*
*a constant reminder to them that you will never leave nor*
*forsake them. In moments when they get weary or afraid,*
*I pray that you would remind them that it takes courage to take*
*a step in the direction of their purpose. I thank you that their*
*Promised Land exists, and you know exactly how to get them*
*there. I thank you that even when it feels like you're not there,*

*you are very present in their situation. I pray that you would help them live boldly, courageously, and unapologetically as the person you've created them to be. I pray that they would no longer dim their light but instead allow for it to shine brightly. I pray they would make daily decisions to be themselves even if it feels uncomfortable. I pray that you would continue to add favor, abundance, and increase to their lives as they journey to and through the Promised Land. I thank you that hell is mad that they've gotten their hands on this book. I thank you for claiming victory over the enemy and for leading them into the Promised Land you created for them to enter. May they forever live Bold & Courageous.*

*Amen.*

# About the Author

**Candace Junée Armour** is an award-winning business coach known for helping women build six-figure businesses. Through her Learn, Market, Grow Digital Academy, Candace Junée has helped over 2,500 business owners increase their visibility, attract paying clients, and make consistent sales through social media. She is also the founder of Epic Fab Girl, a membership and media company that equips Christian women entrepreneurs through Go-Getter conferences & podcasts.

Candace Junée's professional career in digital marketing began as a digital marketing technology consultant & UX Product Manager at Accenture. Before quitting her corporate job in 2017, she helped streamline digital marketing strategies for billion-dollar brands across industries ranging from computer software, fast fashion, media, to technology.

Candace Junée has been featured in Glamour Magazine, Essence Magazine, xoNecole, Rolling Out Magazine, BlogHer, BYOBlive, BAUCE Magazine, WGN-TV and more. Her clients and partners include the Obama Foundation, ManyChat, the NAACP, SamCart, Thinkific, Industrious, Smartwater,

Coca-Cola, Fabletics, Marriott, and more. Candace Junée was named top social media expert by Later Media, and honored as 100 Voices of the Year as a Business Expert by BlogHer in 2020.

Candace Junée graduated with honors from Washington University in St. Louis with a degree in Mechanical Engineering and an MBA with a focus on Marketing & Accounting. While there, she joined Alpha Kappa Alpha Sorority, Inc., and served as the Chapter VP of the National Society of Black Engineers.

Candace Junée has created a life she loves by defying the odds and charting her own path in male-dominated industries. Her new book, *Bold & Courageous* teaches women to show up with authority as the confident experts they are.

# Connect & Free Resources

I'm so sad this book had to end, but the fun isn't over! Ready to continue the journey of becoming more *Bold & Courageous* daily?

I've got two amazing resources just for you. This is just a special thank you for grabbing a copy of my book!

You can get access to both resources at **TheBoldAndCourageous.com**!

Grab your FREE download of *Bold & Courageous* Affirmations which includes affirmations you can speak over yourself daily.

Get access to an exclusive *Bold & Courageous* video training to inspire and encourage you to live as a more *Bold & Courageous* version of you!

If you're looking to grow your brand and business or desire to have me speak to an audience of individuals who are ready to become more *Bold & Courageous*, connect with me online at **CandaceJunee.com** or **EpicFabGirl.com**.

It's not goodbye, it's see you later!

xo,
*Candace Junée Armour*